A Very Short, Fairly Interesting and Reasonably Cheap Book About Studying Criminology

A Very Short, Fairly Interesting and Reasonably Cheap Book About Studying Criminology

Ronnie Lippens

Los Angeles • London • New Delhi • Singapore • Washington DC

© Ronnie Lippens 2009

First published 2009

Apart from any fair dealing for the purposes of research
or private study, or criticism or review, as permitted
under the Copyright, Designs and Patents Act, 1988, this
publication may be reproduced, stored or transmitted in
any form, or by any means, only with the prior permission
in writing of the publishers, or in the case of reprographic
reproduction, in accordance with the terms of licences issued
by the Copyright Licensing Agency. Enquiries concerning
reproduction outside those terms should be sent to the
publishers.

SAGE Publications Ltd
1 Oliver's Yard
55 City Road
London EC1Y 1SP

SAGE Publications Inc.
2455 Teller Road
Thousand Oaks, California 91320

SAGE Publications India Pvt Ltd
B 1/I 1 Mohan Cooperative Industrial Area
Mathura Road, New Delhi 110 044
India

SAGE Publications Asia-Pacific Pte Ltd
33 Pekin Street #02-01
Far East Square
Singapore 048763

Library of Congress Control Number: 2008934311

British Library Cataloguing in Publication data

A catalogue record for this book is available from
the British Library

ISBN 978-1-84860-141-3
ISBN 978-1-84860-140-6

Typeset by C&M Digitals (P) Ltd, Chennai, India
Printed in Great Britain by Athenaeum Press, Gateshead
Printed on paper from sustainable resources

Dedication

This book is dedicated to
Hans, Greta, Erin, Yoran, Lunar, and Arden Hofman,
and to
Peter, Mirèse, and Jonas Colle

Contents

Preface

This book, in its own little way, aims to address the current dearth of philosophical introductions to the study of criminology. It is written for students who have just embarked upon the study of criminology or related fields and disciplines (e.g. law and socio-legal studies, sociology of deviance, criminal justice and justice studies) and who want to familiarize themselves with a number of basic philosophical ideas and insights in order to sharpen and develop their critical abilities. Students who have already progressed into their academic curriculum might also benefit from reading this book. It is my silently cherished hope that even the more advanced criminology student will be able to find, in this little book, reasons to review, adjust and perhaps modify their opinion or position on the issues of crime and crime control.

An attempt was made to make this book as accessible as possible. The number of notes and references has been limited to a necessary minimum, while a 'Further Reading' signpost placed at the end of the book should offer the more inquisitive student an opportunity to expand their philosophical and criminological horizon. Although this is a slightly philosophy-oriented book, great care was taken to avoid as much jargon as possible. Philosophical concepts and ideas are introduced carefully and gradually.

Students without any prior knowledge of philosophy, or indeed criminology for that matter, should be able to grasp the argument in this book without any trouble. However, readers are advised to read all chapters in sequence. The basic argument should then gradually fall in place. Allow me to phrase this differently: readers could do worse than read the more theoretical and slightly abstract chapters (i.e. Chapters 2 and 3 in particular) before moving on to the more concrete and applied ones (4, 5 and 6).

Over the years I've had quite a few interesting discussions with fellow criminologists and legal scholars on the topic of undergraduate education in criminology and socio-legal studies. Colleagues at Keele University and elsewhere have always been very keen to discuss such issues with me. Many thanks go to all of them. I would very much like to mention Anette Ballinger, Lieve Gies and Tony Jefferson in particular here. I really enjoyed the many conversations we had on a whole range of teaching related topics. Last but certainly not least I wish to thank undergraduate criminology students at Keele University, especially Rachel Burns, Matthew Condick-Brough, Randhir Jutley and Kade Morton, for keeping me on my toes during tutorial seminars.

Many thanks to Caroline Porter and Sarah-Jayne Boyd at Sage.

Ronnie Lippens
Professor of Criminology
Keele University
June 2008

A Slightly Philosophical Introduction to the Study of Criminology?

▦ about the book

This book is not meant to be read as a criminology textbook proper. In fact, it is not even an introduction to criminology. What it *does* provide is a slightly philosophical introduction to the study of criminology. The reader won't find any systematic overview or analysis of criminological perspectives and theories in this book. Nor does the book include extensive applications of such perspectives and theories to a number of issues and topics that are often considered to be part of the field of criminology. These include, *inter alia*, the causes of criminality and crime; the form, spread and distribution of crime; the workings and functioning of the criminal justice system; life in prison; the impact and effects of particular forms of punishment on convicted offenders and on society more broadly; the ongoing search for more effective, more efficient and more ethically justifiable or acceptable alternatives to the criminal justice system as we currently know it, and so on. To be sure, some of these issues and topics, and some of the more theoretical perspectives and models with which criminologists tend to study and analyse them, shall be touched upon in this short book, e.g. in order to illustrate a basic philosophical idea or tenet. However, since this is no criminology textbook proper, the reader should not expect a systematic overview. Readers who are interested in a more systematic overview of, and introduction to criminological perspectives, theories, issues and problems could do worse than consult the 'Further Reading' section placed at the end of this book, where a few very good introductory texts are signposted.

As a philosophical introduction to the study of criminology, the book at hand aims to provide those who *intend* to study criminology with a number of fairly basic, indeed *philosophical* ideas and insights which may help them to acquire the critical tools necessary for them to orientate themselves in the vast criminological landscape. But that of course does not absolve us from having to trace the broad outlines of this criminological landscape first, that is, before we embark upon our more philosophical endeavour proper. What is criminology? What is criminology about? What kind of questions do criminologists ask themselves? Let us first say a few words on this.

about criminology

You could do the test yourself. Asked any of the aforementioned questions many, if not most will be inclined to respond by defining criminology as the scientific search for answers to the question, 'Why do people commit crime?' Some may even state that criminology is all about finding the causes of crime. In a way such definitions are not entirely incorrect. Historically, criminologists have, since the inception of their field of study during the latter half of the nineteenth century (the very word 'criminology' surfaced during the 1870s), preoccupied themselves with the *aetiology* of crime. The aetiology of crime is about the search for the principles underpinning the causal dynamics of crime. In short, it is about the 'causes of crime'. The phrase 'causes of crime' however betrays a view of crime as the more or less mechanical effect of a particular set of causes. The phrase suggests that if and when there is a certain constellation of 'causes' present, crime will follow, almost mechanically. If A (a particular constellation of causes), then B (crime), as it were. It would be hard to deny that many criminologists, particularly those working during the early days of the criminological enterprise, did indeed adopt a certain measure of mechanistic reasoning in their aetiological work. I have used the word *mechanistic* here because the 'If A, then B' kind of reasoning is often found in disciplines such as engineering (if button A is pressed, then machine B will start), physics (if A: the object is dropped, then B: gravity will pull it down with a speed of 9.81 − (R+M) m/s), or biology (if A: an infectious disease decimates the population of animals of prey in a given biotope, then B: this will in turn have a detrimental effect upon the predator population). Mechanistic cause–effect forms of aetiological reasoning in criminology might then sound as follows: if in a person is combined a particular set of social (e.g. poverty), psychological (e.g. aggressiveness) and physiological (e.g. hormonal imbalance) factors, then they are bound to commit criminal offences. On a more aggregate level mechanistic reasoning tends to sound like this: if in a particular society levels of social inequality are on the increase while institutional provisions are crumbling away then crime rates will rise.

The question however arises whether such reasoning fails to take into account the complexity of human beings, indeed of *human being* as such. Later generations of criminologists would gradually abandon mechanistic aetiology, as it became clear that human beings and their behaviour and actions could hardly be reduced to mere mechanical causes and effects. Human beings are no mere machines. They are no mere biological organisms. They could hardly be reduced to mere physical phenomena. There is something about human beings, indeed there is something about being a human being, that makes us creatures who have somehow gone beyond (in other words: who have *transcended*) the more or less mechanical cause–effect world of physics and biology. With human beings, the As are not necessarily always followed by the Bs. Human beings have an innate capacity to reflect upon their position in the world. They have this capacity to think about their past, their current position and their future. Human beings have the capacity to attach *meaning* to their experiences; in other words, to *interpret* them in particular ways, and to base their actions on these interpretations. What's more, human beings are very likely to interpret their experiences in diverging and often highly unpredictable ways. Mere physical objects (such as rocks and clouds) or biological organisms (such as plants, viruses, squirrels and pigs) do not possess this human capacity. They live largely in a world of causes and effects, or at least they do so to a greater extent than humans. We humans live in a world where our being a human being – our capacity to reflect upon ourselves and the world around us, and to attach meaning, to interpret, and to act on this interpretation – is placed squarely and firmly inbetween any causal A one might wish to detect and any possible effect B.

Many a criminologist came to realize this soon enough. After the Second World War most mechanistic forms of reasoning were already on the wane. Let us illustrate this point. Most sociologists and criminologists (e.g. Young, 1999: 8–9) would now agree that there is no direct causal connection between levels of absolute deprivation (A) and crime (B). It is not because I am terribly poor and forced to live in a boarded shack that I am necessarily going to prey on others. If everybody else I know lives under the very same conditions, and if I'm incapable or unable to imagine a different way of life, or a way out, then I am likely to choose to resign myself to my 'fate'. If however I live in a stone-built house, but am constantly confronted with others, whom I do not perceive to be particularly more deserving than myself, who live in palaces, or worse, who are scrounging 'shamelessly' off 'my' tax contributions, then I might perhaps begin to contemplate the 'unfairness' of it all. Who knows, I might even begin to plan actions, some possibly illegal, in order to somehow redress the situation.

Moreover, any such perceived *relative deprivation* in itself may not necessarily lead *me* to embark on a crime spree. On an aggregate level that could very well be the case: at a time or in a place marked by high levels of *relative* deprivation (the deprivation perceived by individuals who compare their own plight with that of others, particularly those who they believe are 'unfairly' privileged) one may reasonably expect overall crime rates to increase. At the level of the individual, however, the connection between perceived relative deprivation and the individual's decision to commit criminal offences is not so straightforward. Human existence, as we shall see in subsequent chapters, is much more complicated than that.

Having said that, it is perhaps wise to stress here that the above does not mean to deny that humans have physical bodies that have certain mechanical features (if you hit someone hard, pain will in most cases be felt) or that humans are biological creatures (clearly, long-term food deprivation for instance will have a serious effect on human behaviour and actions). However, what *is* claimed above is that human beings are not *just* physical or biological, or indeed mechanical creatures. Their *being* involves much, much more. In the human world, that is: in the world as it is lived and experienced by humans, for any constellation of causal factors A–A'–A" to be able to produce, in human beings, a particular constellation of effects B–B'–B", they must first pass through the typically human, and between individuals often differing, filters of interpretation, reflection and meaning. Anyone interested in finding answers to the question, 'Why do people commit crime?' should constantly bear this in mind. That's why in Chapters 2 (*on Human Life*) and 3 (*on Human Existence*) we will make an effort to flesh out this issue of what human beings are about, and what human *being* implies and entails. We shall have to introduce, in Chapters 2 and 3, a number of philosophical ideas in order to be able to do just that. There are many philosophical perspectives and theories available to us, but in this book the focus will be on a particular strand of philosophy, i.e. existentialism (Jean-Paul Sartre's in particular) and its precursor philosophy, let's call it proto-existentialism (here we'll be focusing on Friedrich Nietzsche's philosophy). Existentialism is the philosophical perspective by which its protagonists have made a serious attempt to think through what it means to be human, or, to put it slightly differently, what it means to be a human being. What does it mean, existentialists ask themselves, to be part of the human condition? Rocks, trees, squirrels and pigs do not partake of the human condition, but we, humans, do. What are the fundamental, very basic features of human existence? It should be clear that without any insight in these matters one may not hope to be able to think adequately about the first criminological question, i.e. 'Why do people – or *some* people at least – commit crime?'

Do read the preceding sentence again. It says there 'the first criminological question'. There must then be other questions which criminologists are or should be interested in. Indeed there are. Not too long after the Second World War, during the 1950s to be more precise, a number of criminologists and sociologists who were working on problems of crime and its control began to realize how crime and its control are inextricably linked. The occurrence, prevalence and spread of crime, for example, cannot be studied without also looking into the nature and distribution of the measures that are taken with an eye on its control. As we shall see later (in Chapter 4), this connection had been made long before the 1950s, indeed long before anything like criminology itself appeared on the scene. The 1950s however did produce a new insight, or better: at that point in time an insight that had remained more or less implicit became fully explicit. The insight is this one: measures taken to control crime, whether taken deliberately or not, can, and often will, make things worse. They may, and often will, increase criminality and crime rates. Sociologists such as Edwin Lemert (1912–1996) came to note that there is such a thing as *secondary deviance* (Lemert,

1951). By that he meant deviancy that is the result of particular ways in which people, or society at large, react against crime. We are all familiar with the tale of the two boys who went plucking apples in the vicar's orchard. Let's call this 'plucking' *primary deviance*. One boy later went on to become himself a successful apple grower and cider brewer. The other boy, however, got caught in the vicar's orchard, was placed in a borstal, met other juvenile delinquents there, grew accustomed to a criminal subculture, learnt a few tricks of the delinquent trade and then decided to choose the path of a career criminal. In other words, at least *some* forms of social reaction against crime or delinquency (e.g. a noticeable punitive attitude towards youthful delinquents, or the placement in a borstal, and so on) may result in delinquents committing yet more offences (which would then constitute *secondary deviance*), all crime reduction intentions harboured or crime prevention aims envisaged by vicars, youth workers, police officers, probation officers, or prison officers notwithstanding.

The boy in the borstal may have decided to go for a criminal career for a number of reasons. He may have done so out of spite and vengefulness. Or because he believed – rightly or wrongly – that in a world which had shown such hostility towards him this was the only option left. He may have decided to wear the label that was stuck on him ('thief', 'delinquent', 'criminal', and so on) as a badge of honour, as some youths choose to do when they are issued with an Anti-Social Behaviour Order or ASBO. Or he may have done so for a number of other reasons or any combination of the above. There are no mechanistic cause–effect relations here either. Particular forms of social reaction such as punitive labelling and exclusion of offenders (causes A-A'-etc) do not necessarily or mechanically lead to secondary deviance (effects B-B'-etc). Much will depend on how the human beings involved *choose* to interpret, reflect upon and attach meaning to their experiences with forms of social reaction such as stigmatization or ostracism. The message, however, from 1950s criminology and sociology of deviance was quite clear: the way people react to crime or deviance is an important element to grasp if one is to develop an adequate understanding of how offenders (who, they too, are human beings) may wish or decide to behave. Their behaviour may often go in directions that are unintended and unwanted by those who did the reacting, whether they be criminal justice officials or not. An age-old question, well-rehearsed among criminologists and their precursors, thus acquired a renewed impetus: 'What should we do with offenders?' Phrased differently, with moral undertones, 'What ought to be done with offenders?' In more general terms, and with an eye on policy (e.g. criminal policy, or economic and social policy) the question might sound as follows: 'What should be done about crime?'

Questions such as these make up the second theme that criminologists tend to spend a lot of time and effort on. Whereas earlier generations of criminologists might have been inclined to answer such questions in more or less principled ways (i.e. based on either theoretical or ideological principles) without much eye for the often deplorable consequences of criminal policies and other forms of social reaction (e.g. the inefficiency and counter-productivity of criminal justice systems), later generations did tend to heed the message from the 1950s. A whole new branch of criminological thinking and research emerged whereby much effort went into thinking through, and experimenting with, criminal justice reform. A number of *critical* criminologists, as they came to be known, even went so far as to claim that the criminal justice system as such, *any* criminal justice system, is beyond reform or redemption. *Abolitionists*, from about the mid 1960s through to the early 1980s, even argued for the dismantling of criminal justice systems, and proposed alternative forms of social reaction against crime. In some cases such criticism went hand in hand with a complete rethink of the aims and goals of criminal policy. A number of criminologists proposed abandoning the more conventional aims and goals such as punishment, retribution, deterrence, or incapacitation, and replacing them with new ones such as restoration (as in *restorative justice* for example) or peacemaking (as in *peacemaking criminology* for example) instead. We will have a closer look at these matters in Chapter 5.

We have now touched upon two basic themes, or questions, on which the criminological enterprise rests. The first: 'Why do people commit crime, or why do offenders offend?'. The second: 'What should be done about crime, and what should we do with offenders? But that's not the end of it. There is a third. This third theme too is one that has been around, albeit implicitly, since the birth of criminology in the nineteenth century. We had to wait until the 1960s though for it to emerge fully fledged from the shadows. Here criminologists ask themselves the question as to why it is that societies (not just ours) have norms in the first place which then are broken or transgressed by offenders. More specifically, 'Why is it that most, if not all, societies have criminal law that may, indeed shall be breached by offenders who are then called "criminals"?, We have, in this introduction, used the word 'crime' regularly. But the question now arises, 'What *is* "crime"?' We know there is a list of behaviours or actions that have, in the course of the years and indeed centuries, ended up on the criminal law statute books where they are defined as punishable crimes. This list, criminologists came to realise during the 1960s, is what it is: a list. It is man-made. At some point in time each of the behaviours or actions on that list did not figure on it, and that even includes manslaughter or murder which, as historians have been able to show, long went unpunished by king or lord if blood-feuds or the payment or exchange of *wergild* between feuding families or clans managed to settle the matter. This custom survived well into late medieval times. But to continue, some behaviours and actions which are currently perfectly legal may, in future, end up on the list of 'crimes'. Take hunting with hounds for example. It was perfectly legal to hunt foxes with hounds in 1992. As a rider or a hunter taking part in such a hunt you would have had no trouble whatsoever with the law. The same behaviour in 2006, however, that is, *after* the enactment of the Hunting Act 2004, will make of you a 'criminal'. In the UK at least it will; elsewhere in the world you may still be allowed to hunt with hounds without any legal problem at all.

But there is more. Some behaviours and actions that used to figure on the statute books as punishable crimes have now been made legal. Take adultery. Or abortion. If you are a UK citizen or resident you should not fear the law too much if you engage in a little adulterous activity. And abortion is now allowed under certain conditions. Women who had abortions, say in 1964, were deemed 'criminal', while those who had them some time *after* the enactment of the Abortion Act 1967 suddenly found they had clean access to proper medical abortion facilities, all perfectly legal. The criminal law is not written in stone. The list of 'crimes', in the UK as elsewhere, will almost certainly change again. This fairly basic insight prompted criminologists to attempt to explain all these changes. Why is it, they wondered, that different societies have different definitions of 'crime', and why do societies change their definitions so often, historically? Criminologists and sociologists alike have in the course of the twentieth century produced a great variety of answers to these questions. It may well be impossible to list, let alone explore those explanations here. However, many, if not most criminologists would now probably agree with the thesis that changes to the criminal law or, more broadly, to social and moral norms as such, reflect the outcome of social and political struggles whereby those sections of the population who have access to the greatest variety of sources of power (wealth, entrepreneurship, organizational strength, social mobilization, and so on) usually manage to have their views reflected in those changes to a greater extent than other, less powerful sections and groups. Let us have another look at the prohibition of hunting with hounds in the Hunting Act 2004. It might not be too far-fetched an explanation that points to the economic decline of the British rural economy since the mid 1980s, or to the dwindling numbers of rural voters in the electorate; to the emergence of a knowledge-based third sector economy; to the crystallization, particularly during the 1990s, of an urban professional core electorate; to a certain willingness in this highly educated core electorate to cultivate particular moral sensitivities and an eagerness to flex their political muscle symbolically; to the constant need on the part of governing elites to take heed, above all, of this important urban professional electorate's wishes and desires; and so on. There is no need though to assume any mechanistic development here. There is no reason to believe that societies that have the above constellation of characteristics (constellation A-A'-A''-etc, if you wish) will inevitably lead to a particular constellation of outcomes (B-B'-B''-etc), which would then invariably include the symbolic humiliation of 'rural toffs' and their leisurely pursuits. Any outcome will depend on how all human beings involved, especially those with direct political and legislative powers, *choose* to interpret, reflect upon and attach meaning to the situation they find themselves in. In the UK, after a long and protracted political struggle, the majority in Parliament ultimately *chose* to outlaw the hunting of foxes with hounds.

███████ about what follows

Let us now recapitulate. Criminology is, briefly put, about three basic questions. Stanley Cohen is among those who managed to summarize them most succinctly: 'Why are laws made? Why are they broken? What do we do or what should we do about this?' (1988: 9). Here they are in a slightly modified form: 'Why do definitions of crime change and vary across time and space?' and 'Why do particular behaviours and even whole groups or populations get to be criminalized in the first place?'; 'Why do people offend against norms, including legal norms such as the criminal law?'; and 'What should we do with offenders or, more broadly, what should be done about crime?'

In what we have seen so far it might perhaps be possible to recognize one fairly fundamental issue that seems to be cutting across all three themes: conflict. Conflict seems to be underpinning processes whereby particular behaviours or actions get to be prohibited and made punishable. Conflict seems to be present, at least implicitly, in processes whereby people decide to transgress or 'offend' the normative boundaries they are confronted with. Finally, more often than not conflict resides in a great variety of ways by which people and institutions (such as the criminal justice system) react to offenders or to crime more generally. But if conflict is of such crucial importance in matters pertaining to crime and its control, then it might be a good idea if criminologists reflected in some depth on this issue of conflict. Suppose we could, as human beings, do away with conflict altogether; would this mean that crime will then subsequently also disappear? Will there then no longer be any need for criminalization, or for criminal policy? Is it possible to actually think of or devise ways of dealing with offenders or with crime more generally that do not in any way rest on conflict? Is it even remotely possible to imagine criminal policy without conflict? And supposing the answer to such questions is a resounding 'No', what then are we to do? What may we hope for? Questions such as these will appear and re-appear in different guises throughout Chapters 2 to 6 and shall in a way provide the common thread in the remainder of this book.

It is possible to reduce criminology's three questions to two. One might perhaps be able to subsume both the question about criminalization and the one about reactions under the more generic umbrella of 'crime control'. The remaining question, i.e. the one about criminal aetiology, we could then, for the sake of argument, call the 'crime' issue. Chapters 2 and 3 will focus on this crime issue. In both chapters we will make an effort, using Nietzsche's proto-existentialist thought and Sartre's post-war existentialism, to see if there are elements, in what one might arguably call the human condition and in human existence, which criminologists interested in aetiology might do well to contemplate. In both subsequent Chapters 4 and 5 the attention gets drawn onto crime control. Since, obviously, crime control is fully part of the human condition and of human existence, it should come as no surprise if some of the insights generated earlier will have effects that spill over well into these chapters. But Eastern philosophies, Buddhism in particular, will also make an appearance here. Not only is there a *family resemblance* (to borrow a phrase from Ludwig Wittgenstein) between Buddhism and (proto-)existentialism, the former actually has been and still is one of the crucially important sources of inspiration for peacemaking criminologists, whom we already have mentioned. In Chapters 2 to 5 then, if you wish, an attempt will be made to provide students with a number of fairly basic ideas and, one might hope, insights which anyone interested in thinking about issues of crime and crime control may find useful. There is also a sixth chapter. Indeed, this 'thinking about issues of crime and crime control' is of course itself fully part of the human condition. The act of 'thinking' is itself inescapably part and parcel of human existence. We cannot then finish this book without saying a few things about this 'thinking' or, in other words, about the production of criminological knowledge itself. The book ends with a short Afterthought.

It should perhaps go without saying that the short space of this book will not allow for an extensive philosophical exploration of the criminological enterprise. However, I do hope that the small selection of philosophical materials gathered here for the purpose of this book will be sufficient to encourage students to venture further afield, on their own initiative and at their own leisure. Eager students may be able to find a number of reading tips in the 'Further Reading' pages at the end of the book.

2

Transgression, Crime and Control

(on Human Life)

▓▓▓▓ becoming

Let us begin by exploring a number of fundamental philosophical insights – Nietzsche's to be more precise. This chapter is probably going to be the most abstract one, but it should make it easier for the reader to understand the arguments developed in subsequent chapters. So do bear with me. The German philosopher Friedrich Nietzsche (1844–1900) was, arguably, foremost among a number of thinkers who, during the nineteenth century, took to task, quite forcefully so, any philosophical view in which it had been assumed since Plato's *Phaedo* that behind the world of everyday appearances lurked a *real* world of pure essences (or Essential Forms, as Plato called them). This Platonic view went as follows: the world as we experience it in our everyday life is a world of appearances. It appears to us as imperfect, chaotic, change and flux. But that's only appearance. Behind this world of appearances is a real world in which pure Forms, pure essences of what appears to us in the world of appearances, dwell. These Forms or essences are fixed, unchanging and orderly. Nietzsche was one of those philosophers who opposed this view. He did so quite firmly in his *Twilight of the Idols* (published originally in 1889). Nothing in life, he claimed, rests on fixed, frozen, unchanging and orderly essence. Reason, for example, is no such essence. Reason has nothing essential about it. Moreover, no amount of Reason will ever be able to get us to any essence at all. Reason will never enable us to trace the ultimate line between whimsical appearance and essential reality. There *is* no such line. If there *is* an essence underpinning life at all, human life in particular, then, Nietzsche argued, it is one that has nothing fixed or frozen, nothing unchanging, nothing orderly, indeed nothing in particular about it. Or, to phrase it somewhat paradoxically, and focussing on human being in particular, the essence of human being is to have nothing essential, to have no Essential Form at all, and certainly not Reason (with capital R). Human being then, having no essential plinth on which to rest, is change, or at least, potential change. This may indeed sound paradoxical: the phrase 'there is no essential plinth on which human being rests' could itself be read as a definition of the 'essence' of human being. Nietzsche on occasion *did* outline 'essential' features of human life, as we shall see below. However, the basic emphasis, with Nietzsche, is on life – and human life in particular – as becoming and change.

Much then in Nietzsche's thought is focused not so much on what *is* in being, or in life. That which *is* in life is only here and now, in this very moment and place. One second from now it will have moved on, and will have changed from what *was* into something else. Being, human being included, indeed life as such *is* not. It is becoming. Life is always on its way. It never *is* as such. It is always on the move. Or, as the subtitle of Nietzsche's intellectual autobiography *Ecce Homo* (published posthumously in 1908) suggests, one is not who one is, *one becomes what one is*. Life, if it *is* anything at all, is change. If Man *is* anything at all, he is *becoming*. Man is potential for change, for newness, for future; or stronger still: man *is* change, newness, future. This is the case both for Man as a species (the human condition is change, newness and future) as for individual selves: the boy who gets caught stealing apples from the vicar's orchard is more than that which we commonly call 'a thief'. His being is his potential for change, newness and future. He is, at least potentially, a great number of future actions, statements, utterances, and so on. Although the boy's potential may not be unlimited, his being, in the very moment of the act, is already on its way to somewhere else. Already he is becoming something else. So it is for Mrs Thompson, who caught him stealing apples. Mrs Thompson is not just all the features and characteristics that we – herself included – perceive to be making up the human being called 'Mrs Thompson'. In the very fraction of a second when we perceive her to be such and so, Mrs Thompson is already on the move to somewhere else. She, like us, is constantly becoming something and someone else.

This notion, becoming, could also usefully be applied to all the things human beings say and do, or produce. Take law, or morality. The criminal law, for example, *is* not. It too is becoming, always becoming something else. The as yet unrealised potential which lurks in it is, already, on the move; it's only a small matter of time before some of it will emerge as change, newness, or future. The same then goes for moral systems, or moral orders: they are constantly moving, and changing. Very often they do so imperceptibly. But moving and changing they do: having come from somewhere, and while we perceive and ponder them, they are already becoming future and, possibly, newness. But this raises the question as to what it is that makes being, human being in particular, change so incessantly, even if we don't always perceive this change or its potential. What is this thing that fuels the unrelenting unleashing of potential and future *forms of life* from existence?

will to power

Building on the work of earlier philosophers such as Arthur Schopenhauer (1788–1860), Nietzsche locates this fuel in will; in *will to power,* to be more precise. Will to power is the fuel of life; it is through will to power that life comes into existence and becomes. Note that the phrase 'coming into existence' and 'becoming' could be used interchangeably here. If a particular form of life or a particular way of being changes and becomes other, then of course this otherness or this newness, if you wish, comes into existence. Without will to power, there would simply be no life. Nothing would happen. Will to power is not necessarily good, or evil. The issue then is not to be for or against will to power, which would be impossible anyway. It is impossible to eradicate will to power. One may fight some of its emanations, but it is impossible to do away with will to power as such. The issue is to recognize will to power at work in all that happens in life, and that includes human life. The issue, as we shall see later, is to use and mobilize one's own will to power creatively; that is, with an eye on *adding* to the world and on bringing newness into existence, rather than use it to slavishly follow current law and morality.

Without will to power, nothing would come into existence. Nothing would become other. There would be no change, no newness, indeed no future at all. In short, there would be no life. Without will to power the boy in the orchard would not have decided to pluck a few apples. Without will to power, Mrs Thompson would not have been in the orchard; she would not have apprehended the boy; she would not have informed the vicar. Without will to power, the vicar would not have made a heartfelt plea to be forgiving about the incident, and to give the boy another chance. Without will to power, Mrs Thompson would not have discarded the vicar's plea; she would not have gone to the authorities to report a 'theft'. And so on. Without will to power Mrs Thompson would not even exist, nor would the boy, the vicar, the orchard, my university, the criminal justice system, books about forgiveness. As said, it is through will to power that newness and indeed life itself come into our world. Human existence is not a collection of immutable essences that supposedly lurk underneath the superficial chaos and change of everyday experience. On the contrary: it is the result of will to power and this will to power, *as* will, always carries within itself potential for newness and change.

However, that does not mean newness or change is inevitable. In other words, will to power does not automatically or mechanically lead to change, or to newness. Not at all: will to power may actually manifest itself, and very often does so, in human actions through which the status quo is sought or intended. If in a particular society, for example, legal or moral rules, or custom and tradition are cherished and left unchanged, then this does not mean that these laws and moral rules, or that this society's traditions and customs somehow express immutable or eternally valid essences. The only thing it *does* tell us is that in this particular society there seems to be a dominant will to power at work that expresses itself in human actions that *will* for the status quo to remain unchanged. It is then the sociologist's (or criminologist's) job to use his or her will to power to find out what kind of will to power or indeed *whose* will to power it is that insists on the status quo. Moreover, claims Nietzsche, more often than not such a form of suppression of the new is the case. As we shall see in subsequent chapters, in more depth, the suppression of particular forms of creativity is the very act on which societies rest.

The word 'creativity' in the preceding sentence refers to a feature of will to power when it produces something new, that is, when it brings newness into existence, e.g. a new way of life. Real 'creativity' one would find, for example, when a person (e.g. Thomas More, in his *Utopia*, 1516) or a group invent a *new* way of life whereby offenders are not so much assessed by what they have done wrong, as by what they may yet be able to contribute to society as a whole. Or when someone, or some (e.g. the founders of the Spartan state in Ancient Greece) envisage a completely new form of communal and civil life based on (e.g. in the Spartans' case) utter, relentless physical and military discipline (Spartans used to systematically kill their children if they were physically weak). Real creativity, though, Nietzsche maintains, is quite uncommon. All societies tend to harbour on the one hand elites (the *masters*) who mobilize a will to power which is geared toward stymieing or even destroying creative will to power and, on the other, the ruled (the *slaves*) whose will to power most of the time wilfully accepts legal and moral rule, whether their masters' or their own. Nietzsche has on occasion lamented humanity's inability to transcend the animal-like herd mentality whereby will to power is used and mobilised – by 'slaves' themselves most vehemently – in ways that stifle creativity and the production of the new. I wrote 'animal-like' herd mentality in the preceding sentence. Cows or gnus are herd animals and they don't know any better. Their herd animal behaviour follows more or less mechanistically, or so we assume, from their being cows or gnus. Humans often behave *like* herd animals because they tend to decide to use and mobilize their will to power in a herd-like fashion. The instruments that are used to that end we commonly know as law (e.g. criminal law, or the informal 'law' or code in a youth gang), morality and religion. All are instruments of non-creativity.

the *crime against life*

This brings us to another crucial Nietzschean idea. Law, morality or religion, according to Nietzsche, are about fixating things, about preventing events from occurring, blocking off alternative ways of life, suppressing creativity, and so on. All these phrases ultimately mean the same thing. As such they represent death. Since all life, human life in particular, rests on will to power which, by definition, has the potential to bring change and newness into existence, or, in other words, to add possible ways of life to life, or add life to life, any manifestation of will to power that subdues this life multiplying potential is actually a *crime against life*. Or some kind of *death*, if you wish. Law, morality and religion, to varying extents and each in their proper ways, prescribe how one ought to live one's life. They force people to stick with what already is, or with what already has been defined and projected as desirable or acceptable. They will put pressure on people to conform to what is – or to what is held to be – the norm. They block off future.

Law, morality, or religion all involve judgment, i.e. the application of a yardstick of normative criteria to concrete human actions in order to assess, evaluate and, possibly, attempt to block them off by means of, for instance, punishment. Philosophers like Nietzsche tend to have a problem with such non-creative features of law, morality and religion. Law, morality and religion may be productive (after all, out of will to power they *do* produce whole societies of masters and slaves) they are also *anti*-productive in the sense that they do not *add* to life. Will to power, Nietzsche continues, should not be used to slavishly accept, follow or adapt to that which already is. It should on the contrary be used to add to life, to multiply life. It should be used to unleash, day after day, a little more of life's potential. Law, morality and religion reduce life's potential and the possibilities therein. The issue, however, is to expand life's potential and make life more complex, varied and rich, rather than impoverish it. Those whose will to power institutes or maintains oppressive legal, moral or religious codes and rule, and those whose will to power is completely spent on abiding by these very codes and rules all commit the crime against life.

▨ *ressentiment*

But why, one might wonder, do so many people use their will to power to invest so much in the maintenance or in the institution of law, morality or religion, either as masters or as slaves? They do so out of resentment (or *ressentiment*, as Nietzsche writes, preferring to use the French word). Human manifestations of the will to power quite often have petty, *human all too human* (to evoke the title of one of Nietzsche's books) origins such as vindictiveness, vengefulness, jealousy, or vanity. Nietzsche on this point (and on this point only) agrees with Blaise Pascal (1623–1662) particularly with the Pascal of the *Pensées* (published posthumously in 1670). Herd-like humans will, for instance, choose to mobilize, in a given situation, their will to power towards conformity to the dominant order out of vanity. This is the vanity that urges humans, dependent as they are on the herd, to *belong* to a herd. This very same vanity, however, could also push their will to power towards dissent and transgression. This is the vanity that pushes humans to shine, and be admired, or feared, by the herd, which, by the way, only underlines their dependency on the latter. It is through such petty but human, all too human decisions that the will to power, inevitable and unstoppable as it is, abounds in its most herd-like, life-denying manifestations. Nietzsche captures all this under the notion of resentment. Resentment is what prompts will to power to flow to the anti-production and non-creativity of legal, moral or religious rule rather than to creativity and the multiplication of life.

Resentment is part of what Nietzsche calls 'slave morality'. The word 'slave' here does *not* refer to real and concrete historical instances of slavery, e.g. 'barbarians' that were put to slavery in Ancient Greece and Ancient Rome, or the trafficking of African slaves between the sixteenth and nineteenth centuries, or modern day forms of slavery in so-called sweat-shops. A 'slave', in Nietzsche's view, is he or she who out of resentment partakes in the crime against life. Slaves are those who, out of resentment, invest in the use of judgment in law, morality and religious rule in order to stifle creativity and block off human potential. Slaves are those who out of resentment institute, maintain or support a

particular piece of criminal law legislation with an eye on eradicating particular ways of life or particular practices. The eradication of the 'posh' rural way of life and the practice of hunting
with hounds may come to mind here. Or the efforts made by
early industrialists and ruling elites to hinder or even criminalize
autonomous and cooperative forms of life. Or think of the more
recent attempts by organized trade unions and ruling elites to
force Western levels of workers' rights and environmental standards onto highly competitive developing economies – all under
the banner of 'justice', 'equality', 'fairness', or 'human rights',
and so on, which provides the former with the added bonus of
being able to claim, somewhat vaingloriously, the moral high
ground. There may be much resentment fuelling the will to
power in a host of modern *isms*, whether left or right, including
liberalism, feminism, socialism, Nazism, fascism, communism,
or anti-racism. In short, slave morality is morality based on
resentment and in Nietzsche's view that would apply to many, if
not most forms of law, morality and religion. That which so
many people think is 'good', i.e. legal order, moral duty, or piety,
ultimately rests on slave morality putting will to power to life-
denying ends.

Anyone who might now be inclined to label slave morality
and *ressentiment* 'bad' rather than 'good', Nietzsche advises to
consider the likelihood that any such labelling would then, in its
own right, constitute an example of the 'bad' practice of judgment which it is reacting against. Judgment, as we have seen, is
the application of an already existing yardstick of criteria (legal,
moral or religious criteria) and could thus never be able to creatively open up life's potential. The issue then is not so much to
distinguish 'good' from 'bad' or 'good' from 'evil'. The issue, in
other words, is not to judge. The issue instead is to move *beyond
good and evil* (to use the title of one of Nietzsche's works) and
to leave such divisions behind, in order to simply create, add to
life, or multiply life.

Law, morality and religion constrain life. They are a crime against life. However, there's no point in complaining excessively about that. To complain, and to keep complaining, will in turn lead to yet more resentment, slave morality, and ultimately to even more legal, moral or religious anti-production. Vengeful slave morality, particularly the kind that has captured positions of legal, moral and religious power, tends to clog up life with all sorts of constraints that, says Nietzsche, will only level down life's creative potential. Better then is to move beyond complaining about constraints and to actually make an effort to get past endless cycles of slave morality. In order to be able to do that one should even go to lengths to force oneself to admit that one *willed* life's current constraints. One should find it in oneself to admit that one willed all this constraint in and of life, all this crime against life. One may have willed it because the constraints emanating from law, morality and religion also provided comfort and security. One may have done so out of fear, or laziness. The point is, says Nietzsche, to admit that one willed it. Such an admission, however contrived, is then more likely to reduce levels of resentment, which, in turn, should also eat away at slave morality and its resulting call for judgmental anti-production. As such, from a Nietzschean perspective, there is no point in playing the victim: it demeans oneself; it tends to lead to vindictiveness and slave morality; it often calls out for revenge under the banner of notions such as 'justice', 'equality', or 'human rights', and it is therefore unlikely to creatively open up human potential or add to life. Nietzsche wants us to readily admit that our suffering from law, morality and religion is of our doing. Whether we are slaves or masters, we willed it. *Our* will to power led us to institute or adopt it. We willed judgment.

If we are to be creative we must first *will* creativity. We could only *will* creativity if first we admitted that we *willed* constraint, judgment and anti-production. We must make an effort to move beyond the complaints and vengefulness of slave morality and start imagining alternative ways of life instead. The longer we keep on complaining about or resisting the law, morality and religion which we are having to suffer, the longer our will to power will be caught up in this effort of resistance and the less we'll be able to use our will to power more creatively. The deeper and fuller a particular form of suffering or constraint manages to grab hold of and exhaust our will to power, the lesser the chances of us being able to look at the issues afresh, from a different point of view, and the lesser our capacity to be creative. Let us illustrate this. If you live on an estate that seems to be suffering under a leaden blanket of boredom (and resulting acts of vandalism), then there is not much point, Nietzsche might have said, in moaning about the lack of local institutions or activities, in fighting the local government for its lack of initiatives, or in resentfully striving for the levelling down of provisions on an adjacent estate. Better is to help organize communal life on the estate yourself, and imagine a number of joint activities with locals, with people from neighbouring estates, as well as with local authority officials.

Moreover, our own views on life, in and during a protracted struggle of resistance which threatens to drain all our will to power, are then bound to reflect that which we resist so vehemently. If, for instance, we invest all our will to power in the fight against what we perceive to be the rigidity of patriarchy we should then not be surprised to find that our own feminist struggle will tend to mirror this very rigidity. If we spend all our will to power in the struggle against what we perceive to be the oppressive inhumanity of bourgeois capitalists, then we are very likely to end up reproducing this very oppressive inhumanity in our communist utopia. There is very little newness and much stasis in such mirrored reversals.

Nietzsche urges us to be 'affirmative' of life instead. One should always, he says, 'say *yes* to life'. One must say 'yes' even to all constraints (all the while admitting that one has willed them). Such *amor fati* (love of fate), as Nietzsche calls it, should not mean one has to slavishly subject oneself to constraints. To the extent that constraints such as legal, moral or religious judgment are crimes against life, this 'yes to life' can and indeed should perfectly well go hand in hand with a cool indifference. One coolly looks judgmental constraint in the eye, admits one has willed it and, with something approaching indifference towards the constraints one has taken note of, one then gets to the imaginative and creative work of adding to life.

life as art

Art, according to Nietzsche, is about creation. Activities that do not create anything beyond the mere reproduction of what already exists, in this perspective, could hardly be called art. Art adds to life. Art is about the imagination and production of *new* ways of life. Many, if not most of those who call themselves 'artists' then, have, from a Nietzschean perspective, nothing artistic at all about them. A life led according to the rules and guidelines and judgment of law, morality and religion is a life that has remained within the bounds of what already exists. There is nothing artful about such a life. It has in no way added to life. It has not multiplied life. Its will to power has not yielded anything creative. Nothing in such a life is done that enriches life, or that expands the range of human possibility. Many if not most human beings decide to live their lives in such a way. They live and breathe judgment and anti-production.

Nietzsche's ultimate creative force is the future superhuman. Even though the human condition is such that it carries within itself the potential to transcend mere herd-like instincts or the constant nagging of spiteful slave morality, we are still far from achieving real creativity. In his book *Thus Sprach Zarathustra* (1883–5) Nietzsche projects a future being (the superhuman) who is only interested in creation. The future superhuman lives a creative life that *is* art, and art only. He (or she) identifies with nothing that already exists, least of all law, morality, or religion. The superhuman has no idols to mimic or worship. He looks up to no-one. To desire something is to be dependent on it. It is to be a slave. Slaves desire. They desire what others have. They desire something that already exists. Superhuman creators do not. They just create. The message to us, mere humans, is to transcend our desires. Love that which is (again: *amor fati*). Say you willed it, but kill your desire in the process. Do not be dependent on your desire.

The superhuman is independent. He does not look up to nor down on others. He is not interested at all in emulating others or their lives. Ultimate creators such as the future superhuman are not wedded to anything or anyone at all. Not to law. Not to morality. Not to religion. Not to others (the superhuman and Nietzsche would, I believe, abhor today's celebrity and consumer culture!). Not to the thing which some call 'truth'. Truth also is only a product of human, all too human will to power. All that presents itself as truth is nothing but will to power dressed up as knowledge. The superhuman is not wedded to a particular cause. Not even to himself: indeed, he who is wedded to himself (e.g. to his own desires, to his own visions about life, to his own way of life, and so on) will not add anything new to life. He who is content to remain wedded to his own self and to the products of his will to power remains in a state of non-creative dependency. A slavish follower (in this case, of his own rules and beliefs), he commits the crime against life.

Nietzsche's projected superhuman gives the impression of living a life of pure creation in splendid isolation. Nietzsche on several occasions claimed that such isolation is a *conditio sine qua non* for there to be any productive creation at all. Many later and current philosophers, including most who are inspired by Nietzsche's work, would be very reluctant to share Nietzsche's view here. One of those Nietzsche-inspired thinkers, the late French philosopher Gilles Deleuze (1925–1995), for example, has written extensively on how creativity only emerges when a variety of different energies coalesce and blend to produce new ways of life, or new ways of imagining life (see e.g. Deleuze, 1995). The meeting and even clashing of different opinions, and cooperation, in his view, are necessary for something new to be able to emerge at all. This is still about adding to life, or about being creative. The new way of life that is envisaged here is still worthy of Nietzsche's predicate 'art'. But 'art', in Deleuze's (and others') view, always, and inevitably so, has to make use of the materials which are available. And so it is with 'life as art'. A life lived creatively, 'as art', *has* to produce newness out of the materials (e.g. visions about ways of life) that are already available. 'Art' then resides in the way through which these materials, or bits and pieces of them, are reshuffled or re-assembled into something new, into something other than that which already exists. In Deleuze's philosophy there is no slavish following or acceptance of that which already exists though. Like Nietzsche, Deleuze sees human beings as *becomings*, full of potential for the new, rather than as mere *beings*. Unlike Nietzsche, though, Deleuze believes that newness emerges through processes of what he calls *becoming other*. This phrase, 'becoming other', captures two meanings simultaneously, i.e. becoming otherwise than the existent (first meaning) is possible only through processes of creative re-assemblage undertaken *with* others (second meaning) and through an engagement with their views and opinions.

In Chapter 3 we will explore the writings of another of the more recent neo-Nietzscheans, Jean-Paul Sartre (1905–1980) who, on this issue, takes a position somewhere halfway between Nietzsche and Deleuze. In Sartre's view, becoming *new* never takes place in a vacuum. Newness always emerges at a particular point in time and space, and does so necessarily out of materials available there and then. But the decision that underpins the creation of newness is one that is taken by individuals in solitude. They may be among dozens of friends whose abundant advice, or warnings, they may or may not heed. But any decision, any *art*ful decision they happen to base on all this advice will be theirs and theirs alone.

doing away with idols

Because of its ubiquity and its dominance in the Western world since about the fourth century AD, Nietzsche reserved much of his sharp criticism for Christianity (most notably in his *Anti-Christ*, published in 1895). In his view Christianity, particularly the doctrine of Saint Paul, constitutes the ultimate crime against life. Geared towards the subduing of all creative impulses in life it is *decadent*, that is, a terminus rather than a new beginning. Thriving on pity and resentment, it epitomizes slave morality. It reduces all human potential to the idol of an unhealthy ascetic ideal. Its will to power is bent on blocking off life.

Now, Nietzsche did not have too much of a quarrel with the Christ himself. He at least *did* add to life. He creatively produced a new way of life and a new way of looking at life. Christ Himself was wary of the rigidity of law and ritual, and lived a life based on inner strength rather than on idolatry. Saint Paul's doctrine, which formed the plinth on which Christianity would come to rest, claims Nietzsche, made a caricature of Christ's teachings by reducing it to the denial of self (which amounts to the denial of life itself) and by urging Christians to embrace what Nietzsche viewed as the resentful morality of slaves.

The life of Christ had more in common with Buddhism, which Nietzsche had fewer problems with. We will later go into more detail on the issue of Buddhism, but here is the place to say a few words on this topic. Buddhism holds that the road to happiness is found only in the relinquishment of all desire, of all attachments to and identifications with idols. If you do not harbour any particular desires, if you do not feel too attached to particular things or even to people, and if you do not have any idols that you feel you must emulate, then you won't easily feel frustrated or disappointed. That in turn will considerably reduce the chances of resentment and slave morality occurring (to evoke Nietzsche here) and will make the likelihood of life-denying imperatives, in e.g. law, morality or religious practice, remote. In Buddhism one is advised to say 'yes' to life in all its manifestations, but to harbour no interest in or attachment to any manifestation in particular. The former depends on the latter, and vice versa. But for all its peaceful and affirmative calm, Buddhism adds precious little to life. Doing away with idols, that is, emptying oneself of the desire to identify with particular objects or people or lifestyles, and so on, is one thing – difficult though it is, particularly in an age marked by what many believe is an excessive celebrity and consumer culture. Creatively adding to life, however, takes more than that.

the tragedy of the human condition

Truth, as we have already seen, is a human creation. All too human, truth, or better, knowledge that presents itself *as* truth, could only be *particular* and partial. No truth could ever be anything more than a *particular* selection of thoughts and words about particular things (including thoughts and words!). This is the case not just because, as some philosophers have been pointing out recently (see e.g. Lakoff and Johnson, 1999), human beings, having the bodies and sensory apparatus they have, are able to produce only *human* truth (and nothing else). It is also the case because all truth will inevitably have to be produced somewhere, at some point in time, out of a particular set of available materials. Moreover, all truth results from will to power. Will to power is how the human world emerges and becomes, and that includes 'truth'. Any superhuman realizes this. Through the voice of his Zarathustra, Nietzsche implores us not to follow knowledge systems – including his own – but, rather, to create them ourselves. It will then be up to others *not* to follow us. Anyone who decides to accept a particular knowledge system for absolute truth should be aware of the fact that this decision is what it is: a human decision to accept and to follow. It is a particular emanation, says Nietzsche, of a will to power. It *is* a particular will to power, i.e. one which decides *not* to create new knowledge, or new truth, but to accept existing forms of truth instead. Slavishly following existing truth, this will to power chooses submission, hoping, perhaps indeed *willing* to gain from it.

Take gang life. The truth, and the law, of gang A, that is, its code, is only that, a code. As such, it is non-creative, anti-productive. It does not add to life. One acts in a herd-like fashion if one decides to slavishly follow this code. Nietzsche urges us not to follow such codes, but to produce new ones ourselves instead. In other words, do not follow the code of gang A, but create a new code, create a new gang (call it gang B) instead. And once you've got this new code B, don't force it – resentfully – upon others. And to those others, Nietzsche says: do not follow gang B, create a new one, C, instead! And so on.

If truth itself is fully immersed in the flow of will to power, then the same goes for values. We have now arrived at a point, says Nietzsche, writing at the close of the nineteenth century, when the legacy of almost two millennia of slave morality should be subverted. Humanity should become – read again: *become* – indifferent to the vengeful crime against life of Christianity, should move beyond the mere peaceful guardianship of life in Buddhism, and ultimately aspire to becoming a humanity of creators and artists of life. This will require a *revaluation of all* current *values*, to evoke another one of Nietzsche's phrases. He himself tried to contribute to this process by laying bare the *human, all too human* origins of human exploits such as truth and value, or law, morality and religion, and by attempting to unmask and uncover their anti-nature and anti-life tendencies. Nietzsche's thought – his own truth, if you wish – has a psychological slant about it. It locates the origins of much that we have learnt to label as 'good', e.g. order, moral duty and piety, in the deep psychological resentment of slave morality. Emerging psychoanalysts such as Sigmund Freud (1856–1939) were influenced by Nietzsche's diagnostic insights into the underbelly of often revered human aspiration and behaviour.

Preparing philosophy for a post-Christian era, Nietzsche's thought aimed to reconnect with the Dionysian element in pre-Christian Ancient Greek culture. Dionysos was the ancient Greek god of wine, and was therefore a life-affirming, rather than a life-restricting god. The affirmation of life is not brought about by slave morality. It requires a *noble* morality, and it is precisely this noble morality which Nietzsche had in mind when he imagined humanity's *becoming* superhuman. However, this process of becoming superhuman, Nietzsche understood, is likely to be a never-ending story. The process of becoming superhuman will never stop. There might be a glimmer of hope if or when enough people realize that there is no absolute authority 'out there', that is, if and when it is realized that all that presents itself as absolute authority is only the result of human, all too human, *particular* will to power. In Nietzsche's well-known phrase: if or when people begin to realize that God, absolute authority par excellence, is dead. If God or any other authority presenting itself as absolute is dead, and humanity has come to grasp this fully, then perhaps a *new dawn* – to evoke Nietzsche's book *Daybreak* – of humanity might break. Later, philosophers such as the Frenchman Georges Bataille (1897–1962) fleshed out this particular point in quite some depth: one is sovereign only if one is indifferent to and able to elude all authority (e.g. in Bataille, 1998 and 1992). But here is the tragedy of humanity: any imagining or image of what being superhuman might look like, like any other human endeavour, or practice, fuelled as it is by will to power, is bound to fall short of superhuman *nobility*. In the very act of escaping authority one builds one's own. All creativity that adds newness to life carries within itself the kernel of an emerging system (an *ism*, if you wish) of law, morality, or belief. As soon as a new way of life is imagined or proposed, the risk of it becoming a law and an order in its own right sets in. It is then only a matter of time before slave morality will start rearing its head, first from *without*, and subsequently also from *within*. Even a superhuman such as Nietzsche's Zarathustra tells us this much when he explicitly and forcefully urges us *not* to follow him, but instead to live our own lives creatively and productively.

Nietzsche called himself a *tragic* philosopher. 'Tragic' here refers to the ability to fully see the abysmal tragedy of life and not to run from it, but look it squarely in the face. A tragic philosopher is someone who understands that life as such is ultimately unstoppable and unfixable. It is impossible to pin it down completely. Life will always find a way to burst forth, to become ever anew, with all its splendour and with all its horrors. Life is 'eternal recurrence'. The force of life is unquenchable. Nothing human will hold or last forever. Becoming is unstoppable. A tragic philosopher is someone who understands this, and who sees this as an opportunity or as an invitation to stop moaning and to start creating, exploring, venturing and changing instead. A tragic philosopher is diametrically opposed to a pessimist, or to a nihilist who would be inclined to reason along the following lines: since the world is unfixable, nothing will ultimately hold; there is then no point in trying anything at all. Nietzsche's tragic philosophy, however, goes as follows: since the world is unfixable, nothing will ultimately hold; there is then all the more reason not to despair but to start creating anew.

transgression, crime and control

All *becom*ing, in a way, and this may sound like a cliché, implies transgression. Becoming is transgression of that which already exists. Human will to power, as we have seen, quite often ends in non-creative, life-denying restrictions and constraints. However, this is not always the case. Will to power sometimes *does* lead to the creation of newness, to the multiplication of ways of life. Such creativity transgresses existent ways or forms of life. It is through transgression, equally fuelled by will to power, that newness (i.e. new ways and forms of life) comes about. Some of those transgressive results of will to power will then end up being criminalized by particular groups whose will to power will lead them to interpret any transgression of the existent order as a threat to be made punishable, or even to be eradicated. This may in turn reproduce or even engender vicious cycles of resentful slave morality whereby on the one hand levels of 'criminalization' will tend to increase but, on the other, will to power will find other, alternative ways to make life burst forth yet again, incessantly really.

We should then be aware of the original creative will to power that is inherent in much of what we would conventionally call 'crime'. This is not to say that such creativity is found *only* in the transgressive will to power that gets to be criminalized. On the contrary. Moreover, much creativity, despite its original transgression, does not incite punitive reaction. Much of what we call 'crime' is in fact not so much brought about by the creative unleashing of life's potential as it is itself an emanation of vengeful, life-denying slave morality. There is nothing romantic about many of the behaviours listed in criminal law statute books. Much in 'crime' follows or is dependent on its own pernicious and predatory codes. Much 'crime' slavishly follows its own 'laws', its own 'moral' systems, its own beliefs. All this was well understood by Nietzsche himself, albeit that he did tend to locate the origins of criminal life-denying predation in the overall levels of human, all too human slave morality that tends to drain human beings' productive life energy away.

If we now consider the reaction against transgression we will find the situation there to be just as complicated. The judgmental and therefore life-denying tendencies in processes of criminalization, for instance, or in other punitive reactions, are often abundantly clear. Yet this should not mean that there is nothing at all within legal or moral order, or within religious codes, that might deserve the name 'creation'. As we will see later the criminal justice system has itself often been the scene of invention and experimentation. One might even go so far as to claim that new ways of life have been invented by a will to power that used the criminal justice system as the location for the imagination of new practices such as victim–offender mediation, or restorative justice, or even radical abolitionist experiments with alternative forms of collective conflict resolution. Life will burst forth, even in such life-denying settings as the criminal justice system. However, let us not exaggerate our optimism here. Many of these proposed reforms, creative as they are, had their origins outside the criminal justice system and, to the extent that they *are* now implemented sporadically within the confining framework of a criminal justice system, they will, in individual cases, severely and conservatively lean towards repairing or restoring an earlier situation, balance, or status quo. In other words, creative energy unleashed in the setting of the criminal justice system is likely to fizzle out in the reproduction of what *was*, or *is*, rather than in the invention of the *new*.

Let us now recapitulate, in a nutshell, what might arguably be called a Nietzschean view on crime and crime control. The incessant workings of will to power produce transgression as well as reactions against any such transgression (leading to, for instance, criminalization, punishment and exclusion of offenders, and so on). Out of the conflict between both movements, human life and human lives change and evolve, indeed become. One of the results of this unstoppable dynamic of change and resistance is the production of 'crime'. Some elements within said transgressions will be labelled a 'crime', and outlawed. Some aspects within efforts to control this 'crime' will in turn spread cycles of vindictiveness, spite and vengefulness. Slave morality thence underpins not only significant parts of crime control efforts, but also much of what we conventionally know as 'crime'. The life-denying, non-creative and anti-productive *crime against life* occurs ubiquitously both in 'crime' and in its control. For as long as one remains in the human condition, i.e. the condition of will to power and of slave morality, this dynamic is set to continue, inevitably, ineradicably. The particular form and modality of crime and crime control may change across time and space, but the basic dynamic is inescapably human. It's human ... all too human. Nothing human escapes its human – all too human – origins, and that applies even to Nietzsche's thought and philosophy itself, as Lou Salomé (1861–1937), one of Nietzsche's closest friends, once, in 1894, famously argued (Salomé, 2001).

One of the most significant philosophers of the twentieth century, Jean-Paul Sartre, developed a philosophical system (it constituted a form of existentialism) in which he made a serious attempt to think through this basic dynamic of, on the one hand, becoming, and, on the other, slave morality. Sartre himself applied his own neo-Nietzschean philosophical system to the issue of crime and crime control, focussing on the crucial importance of conflict in both. It is to existentialism (Sartre's in particular, e.g. in Sartre, 1943 and 1946) that we now turn.

3

Understanding Crime

(on Human Existence)

▨ existence

In the opinion of Sartre (1946) himself, one of existentialism's basic tenets is this one: *existence comes before essence*. This phrase has now become a pop-philosophy one-liner which some teachers have been known to quite happily evoke in the classroom. You will have heard that phrase before and perhaps you have wondered what is actually meant by it. The phrase suggests, among other things, that human existence is open-ended. There are no fixed and pre-determined goals which human existence is inexorably heading for. But the phrase says more than that. The past, or history, has, ultimately, no absolute hold on the future. That means that although past events or past experiences *are* important, they in no way determine future outcomes in any absolute or fixed way. This refers to what we touched upon in the Introduction: when it comes to human existence, nothing ultimately happens mechanically; nothing is a mere matter of causes and inevitable effects. It's not that because Eric, when he was little, was seriously abused and neglected by his parents, that he is now destined or programmed to end up in a mental health institution or in a youth offender institution. To be sure, some, indeed many abused children do. That, however, is by no means written in stone. It is no 'if A then B' law of human existence. Human existence is much more complicated than that and mere laws of physics (and mechanics) are unable to capture what human existence is about.

At the heart of human existence lies indeterminacy. Nothing is written in stone beforehand. If, at all, there *is* something unmovable or unchangeable, something fixed, or something 'written in stone' in human existence, then it is so because human beings *wished* for it to be so, and have *decided* to make it happen such and so, and to *keep* it that way. The words 'wish', 'decided' and 'keep' in the preceding sentence should indicate how human existence is precious little to do with unshakable essences. It *becomes,* largely through will and decision, rather than through a mechanics whereby particular causes *cause* particular effects.

There are lots of Nietzschean echoes to be noted here. The phrase *existence comes before essence,* then, means that human existence is at its very core indeterminate existence. If there *are* fixed essences to be noted, then this is because we *choose* to perceive them that way. If there *is* an essence called 'Mrs Thompson' then this is not because there really *is* such an essence, fixed and stable and unchanging at the very centre, but, rather, because we, as well as Mrs Thompson herself, choose to believe there is such an essence. These alleged essences emerged out of that which lies at the heart of human existence, i.e. indeterminacy. It is this very indeterminacy through which human beings fabricate 'essences' which they then choose to *perceive* as such. It is through the very indeterminacy which lies at the heart of our human existence, and Mrs Thompson's, that we and she herself chose to act and interact in particular ways, making Mrs Thompson who or what she is today. It is this very indeterminacy which allows us to choose to perceive Mrs Thompson in a particular way (e.g. as being spiteful and grumpy). It was never written in the stone of the laws of nature that Mrs Thompson was going to *be,* or going to be *perceived* to be this grumpy person. All this came about through will, through choice and decision. Thousands and thousands of acts of will, choice and decision have brought us to this point now. And since nothing is written in stone, the very indeterminacy through which all this will, all these choices and decisions took place (if all *was* written in stone, there would have been no will, choice, or decision) will allow for thousands of further choices and decisions. Perhaps these choices and decisions will, in future, leave us with a Mrs Thompson, and with our perceptions of her, that are very similar to those we have today. If or when that happens, it's going to be as a result of thousands of choices and decisions, *not* because of a law of nature, and *not* because Mrs Thompson was, is, and will always be this grumpy and spiteful person. More likely though our future choices and decisions will lead to a different Mrs Thompson, or will lead us to perceive her differently. Human existence is existence of becoming. Human being is becoming. Human existence, becoming, comes before any possible essence. That goes not just for humanity as such (humanity is always on the move), but also for human *beings* individually, and not just Mrs Thompson.

from survey to action

All human beings – you and me included – are always situated in time and space, every single minute or second of the day. This means that each of us is always situated in a particular context, and this context, like any context, is not the whole universe. At every single minute or second of the day we are exposed to and have access to only a limited amount of available impressions, resources and materials. We are always situated in a *particular* context. Never will it be possible for human beings to find themselves in a place where they have access to all possible impressions, all possible resources and all possible materials. We are only human, all too human. Now if we add up all seconds and minutes of a lifetime, or, phrased somewhat differently, if we add up all the contexts we have been in or have experienced, and if we add to that all the possible contexts we have been able to imagine ourselves, we should end up with a pretty impressive amount of imagination and experience. However impressive though, it would still only represent a tiny, almost unmentionable speck in the infinite ocean of all possible experiences and imaginings. Human beings are fantastically limited. Let us now return to that one single second or minute I mentioned earlier.

Every single second each human being finds him or herself in a particular context in the world. Allow one more preliminary remark here: we are talking about those seconds during which human beings partake in the human condition, that is, those seconds in which they transcend their mere physical or biological being. That would exclude any situation where or when they are not in a position to make conscious choices and decisions (e.g. when asleep, or unconscious). What happens in that second? In that second this human being surveys his or her *being-in-the-world*. This survey will lead to a number of impressions being selected and interpreted. This selection and this interpretation do not constitute a mechanical process. This too is a process which at its very core has choice and decision. Once this selection and those interpretations are ready and available, they will then be deliberated upon in a process of *internal deliberation*. This is a process whereby the self deliberates, or reflects upon what it perceives, imagines and interprets, and so on (the word 'self' here needs explication; I'll be revisiting this in due course). After this process of internal deliberation the self may choose to make a number of particular choices. It may choose not to make any particular choice, or decision. It may, in other words, choose *not* to choose. But choice, or decision, there will be, always and inevitably. Based on this choice, the self may then choose – choice again – to take a particular course of action, and then act upon it. There is a lot of deliberation, decision and choice going on here, all in just one second.

Let us focus on this survey of our being-in-the-world or, in other words, our being in this very particular context, in this very second. What is the self surveying exactly? The self surveys what it perceives (better: what it *chooses* to perceive) to be the actual circumstances at this particular time, and in this particular place.

But that's not all. The self also surveys *itself* in its surroundings. It surveys its own past. It surveys others, present and absent, and what these others say and do, how they act. It surveys what these others *might* say and do, if the self acted in this or that particular way. The self surveys what these others, whether present or absent, *might* be thinking about the self. It surveys its own plans and projects for the future. All these materials, or at least a selection, then get to be interpreted or re-interpreted during a process of internal deliberation. The self will, for example, reflect or deliberate upon possible ways in which it might or might not say or do something, taking into account a number of elements. Those elements may include e.g. its perceptions of how others may have perceived previous actions by the self (we are, after all – remember Nietzsche – herd-like beings, always keeping an eye on the herd); or projections of how they *might* react if a particular action was undertaken or a particular sentence was uttered; or contemplations on how one wishes (or not) to change how one comes across to others in the light of one's plans for the future and the image one wishes to project; and so on. The whole being of the self is potentially involved in these deliberations: past experiences, present impressions, future plans and aspirations, perceived practical necessities, knowledge and cultural resources, aesthetic and moral preferences, and so on. All these minute deliberations may indeed take place within one very short second, second after second. Most deliberations will then result in a choice or decision, or in a particular set of choices and decisions. The outcome of these internal deliberations though, or the nature and contents of any choice made, or decision taken, is not written in stone. All choice, ultimately, is made in utter indeterminacy.

The context which a surveying, deliberating and choosing self finds itself in – every single second of its human life – is only that: a context, i.e. a set of elements that are present with (*con*) the text of the self's deliberations. It does not determine anything absolutely. No choice or decision made by a human being has ever been fully and completely determined by the context it was made in. The context is only a limited set of impressions, resources and materials which are available for the self to survey, select, interpret, ponder, reflect upon and base choices upon. There is always choice. That means: there is always a measure of indeterminacy. It is indeterminacy, or openness, which *forces* people to choose, however paradoxical this may sound. Through the making of choices human beings, however, reproduce the indeterminacy that lies at the heart of the human condition, and that therefore also lies at the heart of their very own self. In the very second of human choice, any human being's choice, nothing is ultimately predictable. That does not mean that nothing in human existence is at all predictable. Statisticians spend most of their career trying to figure out the likelihood of particular outcomes (e.g. burglary) from sets of what they would call 'independent variables' (e.g. lack of institutional support in neighbourhoods, significant levels of social and economic inequality, and so on). Their work however produces likelihoods and percentages on aggregate levels, based on data gathered *after* the fact. At the level of the individual surveying, interpreting and deliberating self, in the very split second of a choice or decision, nothing is written in stone. Existence comes before essence. Essence is what we make through choice in the openness (relative openness but openness nevertheless) of human existence.

life project

Choice is always made in utter indeterminacy and openness. Human beings constantly and incessantly survey the materials which are available to them, interpret them, contemplate them, and base their choices and decisions upon them. They must choose. Human beings must make decisions. Every single day they must. Every single minute or second of the day they must make choices. Most of these choices and decisions are of course made spontaneously, but the issue here is to realize that, whether spontaneous or not, choices and decisions they are. Every single choice or decision is different. Each is taken in a process of surveying, interpretation and deliberation which develops in a different context, in a different situation, even if there are only a few moments separating one situation from the next. A few mere moments is all it takes for human beings to *become other*, changed. The very moment in which the self, after a bout of surveying, deliberation and decision, moves from one situation to the next, everything will have changed: the self, the way it interprets its situation, the situation itself ... everything will have changed, prompting another cycle of survey–deliberation–decision. And so it goes on and on. Human life is *that* complicated.

All human beings of course, during their lifetime, go through their own individually singular chain of minute decisions. No two people follow the exact same trajectory, which means that no two people have, at any given moment in time, the exact same 'baggage' of past experience and future plans. No two people will therefore ever find themselves in exactly the same situation, nor will they survey, interpret, deliberate or decide any given situation in exactly the same way. There is more. Since each individual self is never exactly the same from one moment of decision to the next, or from one situation to another (the self is always *becoming*) one might assume, at least theoretically, that in each singular moment or situation in which the self decides and chooses, it should then always have to go through the survey–deliberation–decision process starting from scratch, so to speak. The indeterminacy at the heart of human beings won't go away. There is no stable, unshakeable core at the heart of the self that would, if it existed, take all decisions in its own particular way, as a machine, or an automaton would.

Sartre's existentialism, however, allows for some consistency across an individual's decisions, but only up to a point. At the very deep kernel of the self, very close to the open gap of indeterminacy which marks all human beings *as* human beings, Sartre writes, resides the self's basic, fundamental *life project*. This refers, as it were, to the self's most fundamental, *original choice*. It includes notions of what kind of human being, indeed of *who* he (or she) ultimately wishes to become. Or perhaps more accurately, this life project comprises basic projections or images of the kind of person the self wishes to be perceived as. Life projects have little detail about them, and many of us are not really aware, at least not constantly, of our own personal life project. Life projects are very rudimentary but will, if not determine or structure, then at least colour, to some extent, the self's choices and decisions as it moves from moment to moment, from situation to situation, giving those choices and decisions a certain consistency. A criminologist who wants to understand why a criminal offender makes the choices he makes, or why a police officer acts in her own particular ways, or why a judge tends to motivate his judgments in his, Sartre advises, should make an attempt to find out about their respective life projects. He calls such attempts *existential psychoanalysis*. Might it not be the case, for example, that the offender chose to become a burglar (rather than a robber) because his original choice, his life project, has something to do with being, or coming across, as self-sufficient, independent, unobtrusive, cool and imperturbable, in short, with being really sovereign (in George Bataille's aforementioned definition). Might the police officer's recurring pleas for the implementation, in her local police station, of an additional victim support unit (to the dissatisfaction of some of her colleagues) have something to do with her original choice, her project to become a sort of authority figure, a kind of *mater familias,* if you wish, who yields admiration and respect (from the herd) by providing them with help and support? Might the judge's penchant for sneering remarks towards convicted CEOs and other 'white collar criminals' be related to his original choice to become a kind of protector of the weak, or a hammer of the rich, thus hoping to acquire elite status which, a son of menial labourers, he never really had ... to become an avenging slave, as it were (to evoke Nietzsche once more).

Seen this way one might perhaps be inclined to conclude that any human being's actions are not so much determined by the past (by past experiences) or by the present (by the characteristics of and materials available in the situation of the moment), but rather by the future (i.e. by future projections of the self in the life project). But that would perhaps be one bridge too far. Indeed, a life project, a person's original choice is what it is: a choice, a decision. As a choice or decision, it has not been able to fully close the gap of indeterminacy at the heart of being. The self has the capacity to decide, at any point in time, to adjust or even radically modify its life project. It often happens: people, unlike mere physical objects or mere biological organisms, *do* have the capacity to change themselves, to create or re-create *themselves* anew, at their very core. In the human world, existence comes before essence ...

alone in freedom

There is no ultimate authority pushing us or dragging us into predetermined directions. Sartre agrees firmly with Nietzsche here. We choose and make our own selves and future out of the materials that are available to us and which we constantly survey, interpret, and deliberate and decide upon. All this, however, begs the question as to how it is possible for human beings to reinvent themselves. What is it that allows the self to do all this;

what is it that allows it to choose? This is so, says Sartre, because at the heart of the human self there is distance and openness. At the very core of the self one finds a gaping *hole* of *nothingness*. This is the nothingness in the title of Sartre's most famous book, *Being and Nothingness* [1943]. It is through this hole that choices are made, and that the self *becomes*. This hole is nothing but the space that is created when the self takes a step back from itself, thereby including *itself* in its survey of its being-in-the-world. The hole that opens up when the self thus monitors itself in its surroundings, surveying and pondering past, present and future, is sheer nothingness. By that Sartre means total indeterminacy, i.e. the complete and utter freedom to make choices. This hole of nothingness and freedom, or, in other words, the distance between the self that monitors itself and the monitored self, is what makes the human self human. Physical objects and mere biological systems do not possess this capacity to monitor themselves (i.e. their own past, present and possible futures), their own actions and those of others, in the midst of their surrounding world.

Since this hole at the heart of the self is a hole of nothingness, of indeterminacy and of freedom, the self is able to contemplate a variety of courses of action, deliberate on their likely consequences, and ultimately make a choice. If there were no such distance or nothingness within the self, or, in other words, if the hole was filled up, then it would be impossible for the self to survey itself within its surrounding world, and it would therefore not be able to freely contemplate its past, present and possible futures. Such a self, in short, would be living out a mere physical or biological life. Its actions would be merely physical or biological, indeed *mechanical* reactions to environmental stimuli. The self would not have the capacity to reflect upon its past, present and future; it would be unable to survey and contemplate the situation it finds itself in; it would not have the capacity to detect a variety of courses of action, nor to decide on making a choice. It would not have the capacity to create itself anew. It would then not be a fully human self.

That which makes human existence possible, i.e. the hole of nothingness at the heart of the human self (without it, there *is* no human existence), is ineradicable. If and whenever the self has the capacity to survey and contemplate itself, then there will be nothingness and indeterminacy, or utter freedom, underpinning the process. The hole of nothingness shall only be blocked off, or filled up, if one leaves the human condition altogether. In the human self, there is always going to be nothingness and indeterminacy at its heart. The human self always, and inevitably so, makes choices. There is no escaping choice. Certainly, a middle manager who has spent most of his working life among colleagues who made corruption their way of life will have a very hard time staying on the straight and narrow. While surveying, every minute of the day, his situation, and contemplating his past, present and possible futures in the light of his own life project and the signs coming from his colleagues, he is bound to experience formidable pressure to join them. There is, however, always going to be choice. If he decides to join them, then it shall be *his* choice. His boss and colleagues may threaten him with dismissal (or worse) if he refuses to join them (such threats could be quite a foolish thing to do in this whistle-blowing age of ours) but still he will have the choice not to give in and perhaps hand in his resignation instead.

There always is a choice. A prisoner, stretched out on the torturer's rack, who, fully conscious and aware, experiences intense pain, always has a choice: either she chooses to betray her rebel friends or she won't. The outcome of her deliberations is going to be a result of a decision taken in freedom, hellish pain notwithstanding. To give one of Sartre's own examples: a thoroughly exhausted mountaineer who is only one step from death will always have at least one more choice before death. Either he decides to stop and rest, and live, or he decides to take that one additional step and die. He may contemplate his life project (e.g. to be a hero was always part of it) before he decides. He may ponder his fellow mountaineers' possible reactions. He may do all this in utter panic. But at the end of this process there's going to be a decision, and a choice, and this decision and choice are going to be his and his alone. There will be friends trying to advise him, or trying to talk him into or out of a decision, and he is in all likelihood going to include all this advice and all these pleas into his deliberations. The process however will end in a moment of choice: to die (a hero's death) or to live (a weakling's life). The choice will be his and his alone.

It is impossible for human beings, *as* human beings, to escape choice. They cannot escape this freedom. However, one should also recognize and admit that many are unable to carry this heavy burden of existential freedom. Many indeed will make every possible attempt to flee from it. The German philosopher Erich Fromm (1900–1980), who was writing his seminal work at about the same time as Sartre was working on his, analyses the ways by which people usually choose to *escape from freedom* (Fromm, 1941). Writing against the backdrop of the Second World War (like Sartre) he explained how modern man in particular, thrown in the midst of individual freedom, and feeling alone as a consequence, often resorts to a number of mechanisms which he hopes will deliver him from both the burden of freedom and the one of aloneness. These mechanisms include sadomasochistic authoritarianism (the exercise of or submission to authoritarian elements), destructiveness (the singling out of enemies which then have to be fought to destruction, time and time again), and automaton conformity (the blind acceptance of and submission to dominant norms and rules). These strategic options provide modern man, fearful and feeling alone in all his freedom, with a way out. Sadomasochistic authoritarianism, war-like destructiveness, and blind automatism all allow modern man to escape his freedom in order to regain a sense of regularity, stability, security and even community. But these options, if we now remember Sartre, are just that: options, which one may, or may not choose to take, or, as the case may be, discard or ignore altogether.

Let us return to Sartre's insistence on choice. Since all choice is ultimately choice made in utter freedom, and in complete solitude, all human beings are responsible for their own choices. This may sound very harsh, but let us have a closer look at this statement. When it is said here that all choices are ultimately made in utter freedom this does not mean that the self always and at any particular point in time could decide to choose from an infinite range of possibilities. It only means that the self, *given* the elements and materials available to it in its present situation, that is, *given* its past, *given* its capacities and abilities, in the light of its imagined futures, and so on, freely decides to choose from the *limited range* of possibilities which it perceives to be available and accessible. But, however limited, choice there is going to be. And *that* choice will be made in utter freedom, by a self that is forced to choose in solitude, even if it is surrounded by well-meaning friends or ill-meaning enemies. Surrounded by tonnes of social pressure, friendly advice and begging pleas, the self, at the very moment of making its choice, is alone. Any choice made will be its own. There is no authority who decides for us. We may not be responsible for the limitations of and constraints in the situations we find ourselves in, but we *are* responsible for the choices we make *in* them. The middle-ranking manager may not be responsible for the fact that his colleagues are all involved in corruption while the CEO encourages all newcomers to do the same; he *is* responsible for the choices he makes given this situation (e.g. either joining or denouncing his colleagues). The local magistrate is not responsible for her intellectual capacities and her social background; she *is* however responsible for the choices she makes within the bounds or restrictions of this given condition. Now, many human beings find it extremely hard to shoulder the responsibility for their own choices, as we have seen. So they hide, or better: they choose to hide. They may choose to hide behind some authority or other for example. Nietzsche's notions *slave morality* and *herd-like mentality* do come to mind here.

bad faith

One of the foremost sociologists of the late twentieth century, Zygmunt Bauman, has analysed how many choose to blindly follow orders, rules or guidelines, thus hoping to be able to shed their own responsibility in the process (e.g. Bauman, 1989). In bureaucracies, for example, many are happy to merely follow the predetermined procedures which in an impersonal manner stipulate how one should act in particular situations. History has shown that a great many people are willing to follow such procedures even if those procedures tell them to commit the gravest atrocities, including, say writers such as Bauman, taking part in the Holocaust. Following such procedures relieves people (or so they believe) of hard-to-bear personal responsibility. They would hide behind authority, any authority (e.g. the one who decreed bureaucratic, impersonal procedure), happily admitting that when they did what they did (e.g. torturing political opponents, treating prisoners badly, and so on), that is, when they made the choices they made, they were only following orders, or procedure. The often unpleasant outcomes of their decision to choose to follow orders or procedure, many believe, are then *not* their responsibility. It is then *not* their fault.

Hierarchical rule and bureaucratic procedures thus tend to provide people with a more or less easy way out of the agony of personal responsibility. As we shall see in the next chapter, systems of hierarchical rule or bureaucratic systems were often devised and implemented with an eye on their capacity to streamline human behaviour or indeed make human behaviour more predictable.

Many gladly make use of the opportunities in such systems, for they offer them a number of desirables. Think of the sense of security that goes hand in hand with predictability, or a certain peace of mind when it comes to making unpleasant choices, or a screen to hide behind when deciding a particular course of action, or an opportunity to avoid having to make uneasy deliberations at all, and so on.

Hiding and fleeing from responsibility is akin to what criminologists Gresham Sykes and David Matza (whom we shall meet again later) once called the *techniques of neutralization* of guilt and responsibility so often used by offenders to justify their actions (Sykes and Matza, 1957). Having committed criminal offences of some kind many offenders tend to deny the criminality of their actions ('It was an accident', or 'Nobody got hurt in the end'), or blame the victims ('He asked for it') or us, their condemners, instead ('This here is class justice, and I'm only a poor working class girl'). But they would also appeal to and hide behind higher loyalties or authorities ('I had to cook the books, your honour, for if I hadn't the firm would have gone bust and workers would have ended on the streets, jobless'). Some may hide behind what they perceive to be their own character ('It's just me!', or 'I can't help it'), which, as existentialists would claim, makes no sense at all, for there is no essential 'I' or 'me'; there's only an endless series of choices made out of a hole of nothingness. Existence comes before essence. Essence, any essence, is a result of choice.

Offenders may also hide behind group pressure ('They made me do it!') or, indeed, hierarchical authority and procedure ('I was just following orders', or 'But it says here in the guidelines that we must deal with even minor infractions very harshly'). All these justifications may, up to a point, betray a certain desire on the part of the offender to remain accepted by or included in mainstream society. They may even have a ring of truth about them. That is not the issue here. The issue is that ultimately the self *chose* to follow the rules and guidelines, ultimately *chose* to act in a very unpleasant way, and ultimately *chose* to try to shed its own responsibility and hide behind authority or behind any other justification instead. The self chose all this by itself. It did so in utter freedom and all on its own, all forms of pressure, real or imagined, notwithstanding.

It may be worthwhile to repeat here that the self deliberates, decides and chooses not just by weighing potential costs and benefits, whether short-term or long-term ones, of any possible course of action. Human being does not come into existence by means of deliberations and choices that are purely 'rational' (the word 'rational' is used here in the sense of 'assessing and weighing costs and benefits' of actions). Human choice is never solely and uniquely 'rational'. When the self surveys its own predicament and its own position in the world before it decides on or chooses a course of action it does so, certainly, with a measure of instrumental 'rationality', but much more is involved in the process, and a lot of it pertains to some extent to the self's original choice, i.e. its life project. Considerations about perceived pragmatic necessity, for example, or aesthetic sensibilities and preference, may all be involved in the said process, as will sheer intellectual capacity and cultural baggage, or the lack of it. Reflections about morality or about how particular actions may make the self 'look good', or as the case may be, 'bad', are also involved. Indeed, sometimes a course of action may be chosen precisely because it makes the self look 'bad', and 'being bad' sometimes *is* the envisaged image which the self wishes to project. Just think of youth who would be very happy to wear their ASBO as a badge of honour, showing if off to their mates. Or the police officer who bends the rules and who boasts and bullies his way through the police organization, because deep down he wants to come across as a 'Dirty Harry' kind of detective. This brings us to the issue of the moral consequences of human choice.

There are no ultimate or universally applicable guidelines that could provide us with complete guidance during our deliberations, decisions and choices. All our choices occur in very concrete circumstances, and even if there *were* very sound or universal rules and guidelines available, we would still have to apply them in every single concrete situation. Since no two situations are completely alike, that means we would still have to go through delicate surveys, considerations, deliberations, and so on, every single time. Of course, as we have seen, most people tend to take the easy road and hide behind the first available rule, order, or guideline. However, says Sartre, who echoes Nietzsche here, no religious or ethical code, no philosophical, psychological or criminological theory will provide the self with hermetically sound guidance as to how to choose. The young man, Sartre illustrates (in Sartre, 1946), who at the outbreak of the war goes to see a priest in order to ask him whether he should join the resistance and fight the invaders, or stay with his ailing mother instead, should not expect to obtain a definite answer to his moral quandary. There is no ultimate authority to sort us out. The self must survey, deliberate, decide and choose in utter freedom and solitude. Others may advise us to put the patriotic love of country before the care of family (or vice versa), but the final and ultimate choice will be ours. Not the priest's. Not philosophy's, not science's. It is nobody else's choice but our own. It is impossible to escape from this human predicament. If we *do* try to escape, or if we hide, for example, if we accept the priest's advice and choose to care for our mother instead of helping the resistance movement (or the other way round as the case may be), but subsequently justify our action before others, who call us to account, by saying that 'The priest told me to do it', or that 'Others made me do it', or that 'The situation was such that I could not act otherwise', and so on, then this amounts to what Sartre calls *bad faith*. Anyone who refuses to take responsibility for his or her decisions and choices (which will have been made in utter freedom) falls into bad faith. Anyone who hides does so in bad faith. Any offender who says 'I was abused as a child and I grew up in a rough neighbourhood, so therefore I automatically became a bully and a robber' falls into bad faith. Childhood abuse, neglect, and an overabundance of violence and aggression may have provided most of the materials that made up the offender's childhood horizon. However, this horizon will also have included other elements or at least the potential for other inter-pretations of one's experiences, for other life projects, for other courses of action. Becoming a bully and a robber was, and is, every single day, a choice. There always is a choice. At the very, very extreme the choice is this one: either I steal a loaf of bread and live, or I don't and die.

This may sound terribly harsh. Some may now be inclined to think that if all the above indeed does make sense, and if offend-ers are ultimately – that is, in a philosophical sense – responsi-ble for the choices they make, as we all are, then they should be punished accordingly, e.g. according to the principle of *just deserts*, or according to another, more stringent or punitive prin-ciple. But how *we* deal or ought to deal with offenders does not mechanistically follow from, and is not determined by, the offender's responsibility. How we – Mrs Thompson, the vicar, the police officer, the magistrate, you and me – deal with offend-ers is *our* responsibility. It is ours and ours alone. We cannot hide behind the law, behind ethical guidelines, behind religion, or behind a popular call for harsh punishment. If a judge says, 'This offender has had a rough time himself, but nevertheless he chose to rob this poor woman at gunpoint, so the *vox populi* as well as the law leave me no choice but to sentence him to 25 years in prison', he falls into bad faith. The judge hides, and cov-ers up his own responsibility. Indeed, he hides the fact that he himself has made a number of choices in utter freedom. He hides the fact that he *chose* to pronounce this particular sentence. He hides the fact that he *chose* not to criticize, much less resist the law, the criminal justice system, or the popular punitive call. He *chose* not to mention the fact that he *chose* not to be interested, much less involved in social and political activities aiming to reduce child poverty or domestic violence. He hides the fact that he *chose* not to mention or consider legal provisions that allow for mitigating circumstances and justifications to be taken into account. He *chose* not to mention alternative and possibly more effective and more efficient forms of non-custodial sentencing, including victim–offender mediation, reconciliation conferences, or other kinds of restorative justice (more on which in Chapter 5); and so on. In short, like the offender, the judge chose not to take responsibility for his own survey, his own interpretations, his own deliberations, his own decisions and his own choices. He made the choices he did, but refused to admit as much. His will to power, to evoke Nietzsche once more, made him choose to run and hide, *herd-like*, instead.

But all choices, including the offender's and the judge's, and yours and mine, have a moral impact in the sense that they have an effect on others. They always and invariably have. If I choose to intervene in a fight between girls who are engaged in a bout of 'happy slapping' on the corner of the street, my choice will have an impact on the girls involved, on their parents, their school, the local neighbourhood, and so on. If I choose not to intervene, my choice will equally have an impact. On a more abstract level our choices, as well as our actions based on them, have another kind of moral impact: they help define humanity in its ever-ongoing process of becoming. To give an obvious example here: if someone decides to invent the idea of an internment camp, or an extermination camp, and then chooses to build one and operate it, and if many choose to support this or look the other way, then these decisions and choices will henceforth help define what it means to be 'human'.

■ dizzying words

Many, if not most people choose to follow or mimic what others do. More often than not, they end up living a life that is built around habits, routines and structured patterns of behaviour. But choice will always be involved. If someone spends most of his or her time following routines, he or she does so by choice. There will be a constant process of survey, deliberation and decision underpinning these endless routines. No routine, no habit – however fixed – will ever be able to stop the self from monitoring its own performance in its surroundings. There will always be this hole of indeterminacy lurking underneath all routine and habit. It will always be possible for the self to decide to change its ways, to do things differently, indeed to *become other*.

As said, most people in most circumstances choose to use the openness in this ever-present possibility to merely follow fixed routines. Now such routines are, more often than not, the result of particular orders or commands, or guidelines, rules and codes of all kinds, or are perhaps just manifestations of habit. One could say that many of those routines derive from a *herd-like* choice, made by the self, to dwell in the safe conformity of a dominant and perhaps uneventful order. Sometimes, however, routines follow an equally *herd-like* choice to take part in rebellion, and to mimic the unsettling habits of the shining few. In both cases nothing much in the way of creative change, invention or newness is going on. But change, creative invention, or re-invention, is always possible. This often happens through shock, that is, when the surveying self suddenly finds itself having to confront new and perhaps unexpected materials. Materials pertaining to the surveying self's relation to its surroundings (and others therein) in particular could and often do bring about a change in the self's deliberations, decisions and, ultimately, its choices. To be called a thief for the first time at a tender age (or at any age, for that matter) may induce such a life-changing shock.

What others say and do, and what they say about us in particular, or what we *think* they think and say about us, are all important materials that our 'self' will be inclined to seriously contemplate during its deliberations. When it becomes clear that others tend to reduce the full complexity of our being, our self, our full potential indeed, to one or only a few characteristics (e.g. 'Thief!'), then this may lead the self to embark upon very significant and often life-changing deliberations. Sartre has on occasion termed such words 'dizzying', for in the vertigo they tend to cause, the self reconsiders all its earlier choices, its future projections, its position in the world and its relation to others, and so on. In some cases this leads to a complete overhaul of one's basic life project. When that happens, the self in a way re-invents itself. Put slightly differently, the self, which always carries within itself the potential for creation anyway, creates itself anew. It may be very hard to predict the outcome of any such process of self-creation beforehand as, of course, it takes place in and through the hole of indeterminacy that continues to lie at the heart of the self.

Sartre has himself made a tremendous effort to illustrate such processes of self-creation in his book on the French novelist Jean Genet. Having read and meticulously analysed all of Genet's works, Sartre, in the book, made an attempt to minutely document the intricate considerations and incredibly complex deliberations which, he assumed, Genet might have gone through after he was caught stealing a few pennies at the age of 11. He was immediately accused of *being* a thief. His whole being was suddenly reduced, in the eyes of others, before the gaze of others, to *being* a thief. The book, *Saint Genet* (1952), is a massive tome in which Sartre, having read Genet's works, imagines in the most intricate detail how Genet might have created and re-created his own life project, his own self, in the decades following this event. Sartre documents how Genet, who, as a foundling, always had worries about other people's perception of him, at first internalizes the label 'thief', making a deliberate decision to *become* a thief. In other words, he chooses to turn the label into his own life project. Attentive readers will no doubt recall here the notion of 'secondary deviance' which we introduced in our Introduction. In later years Genet goes on to re-invent himself again and again, first as a prostitute, then as a successful poet and novelist, and later still as a renowned international journalist. None of these re-inventions of self could have been predicted. None of this was written in stone. Genet became anew through indeterminacy. It was indeterminacy that allowed him, time and time again, to contemplate his interactions with others and to reconsider his relation to them. It was indeterminacy through which he re-invented himself. Indeterminacy is what allows human being to come into existence.

Sartre's work here shows quite a few similarities with a strand of sociological thinking which emerged in the US roughly between 1900 and 1940, i.e. interactionism (later called symbolic interactionism) whose foremost theorist and proponent was George Herbert Mead (1863–1931). This sociological perspective would later become very popular among criminologists. At its most basic level symbolic interactionism holds that human life is thoroughly social in that it is shaped in and through very minute interactions between individuals and groups. At the heart of these interactions symbolic exchange takes place. Put more simply: during interactions people tend to use and exchange gestures and words. Sometimes words are used to 'label' particular events, or groups, or behaviours, individuals or, more generally, situations. In other words, people will *define the situation*. Now in many cases there is a broad consensus about this labelling, or about these definitions of the situation. That is by no means the case all the time. Depending on their point of view, or perspective, people may differ on the applicability of particular labels or definitions. Some may choose to label unrest or agitation in the street as 'a long overdue pre-revolutionary climate', while others will be inclined to label the very same unrest as 'despicable actions of work-shy hoodlums'. A boy plucking a few apples in the vicar's garden may think himself to be engaged in the most innocent of pastimes but, as we know, Mrs Thompson would beg to differ; she calls out 'Thief!' at the top of her voice without the slightest hesitation. All labels somehow define the situation, and all definitions of the situation are reductive. By that is meant that all such definitions (whether positive or negative, supportive or not) *reduce* the full potential of that which is labelled or defined (an event, a person, a group, an act or behaviour, and so on) to only one or a few aspects. Most of the time people won't mind. However, sometimes people *do* mind, or, at the very least, are shocked by the label, or by the definition.

This is particularly the case when the label goes firmly against its target's life project, or against the image he or she wishes to project towards others. Young Jean Genet might have been in that position. The target self who, like Genet's, receives a *dizzyingly* negative label may feel prompted to undertake a thorough contemplation of its whole being, or better, its whole being-in-the-world. Mead (e.g. 1934), like Sartre, distinguishes two parts in, or dimensions of, the self. There is the monitoring part (the 'I') and the monitored part (the 'me'), monitored with an eye on how we think others might perceive us; monitored, if you wish, through the eyes of others. During such contemplative *private conversation* with itself (again note the similarities with Sartre's existentialism) the self may consider a number of possible avenues or options, and will ultimately make a decision.

Such decisions, as we already know, are unpredictable. They are the uncertain outcome of indeterminacy. But at some point decision there will be. The self, in a way, will itself then also define the situation. The self, in other words, may then in turn attach its preferred meanings to the label and base its actions,

and possibly even its re-invented life project on its own definition of the situation. Called a thief, with its being reduced by
others to simply being a thief, rather than respected as an innocent lover of fruit and vegetables with lots of potential, a young
boy's self could then for example define the situation as follows:
'I am under attack. Those who call me a thief got it wrong.
However, since I am under attack, the best defence is a counter-
attack. If they want me to be a thief, then thief from now
onwards I will be. Who knows, I may even get admired for it by
my mates'. The original definition of the situation, i.e. the application of the label 'thief', will then have been a *self-fulfilling
prophecy*. Or let us take an example provided by Sartre himself
(in Sartre, 1946). A young woman is deemed to be irascible by
her in-laws, who unwittingly act upon their definition of the situation, leaving her to interpret their behaviour as hostile.
Contemplating all this, and not wishing to come across as a silly
goose (which would not match with her life project and future
self image) she starts behaving aggressively, and gets effectively
labelled 'irascible', which in turn prompts her to define the situation as 'more hostility' and so on.

But not all labels are self-fulfilling prophecies. The self's reac-
tive definition of the situation may go like this: 'They're right. I
do need to get my act together. I'll apologize and make good.
They're not bad people at all, and I do cherish their company'.
And so on. The nature of the self's own definition of the situation is hard to predict with unwavering certainty, particularly in
cases where the self is seriously scrutinizing and contemplating
its own life project.

Having defined the situation, the self may then choose to act
upon it in particular ways. This will prompt others to survey the
self's reactions in turn and to contemplate them, attach meaning to
them, define the situation created by them, and choose a particular course of action. This never-ending chain of actions and reactions, or social interaction in short, is how human life takes shape

and develops. It takes shape reduction after reduction (see also Schinkel, 2009). The outcome is, at any given point, uncertain.

It should be clear that language is of crucial importance here. Since language inevitably reduces the fullness of being or the potential which is present in situations, or in people, to one or only a few aspects, there always is, in human interaction, ample room for the interacting parties to doubt each other's genuine intentions, to misunderstand each other, simply disagree, enter into or prolong conflict. Language, inevitably reductive, *is* important. This is why some abolitionist criminologists (whom we have already mentioned in the Introduction) tend to show great sensitivity to the very use of words such as 'crime' or 'criminal'. If, they argue, one defines a particular situation as 'crime', or a particular person as 'criminal', then a host of particular consequences is likely to follow in the wake of such definitions. The infliction of additional suffering in and through the workings of this thing called 'the criminal justice system', for example, which, abolitionists argue (e.g. Hulsman, 1986), is ineffective and counterproductive; better then is to call unwelcome situations or events 'problematic situations'. This label is less reductive, that is, it does not pin down situations or people onto fixed and frozen positions, and if it does, it does so to a lesser extent. Such language also allows for a more extensive exploration of alternative ways of dealing with the 'problem'. Indeed: 'problems' require 'solutions', while 'crime' merely evokes 'punishment'.

existentialist criminology

There is currently a body of criminological literature (e.g. Crewe and Lippens, 2009) emerging that, inspired by existentialism, analyzes how minute and intricate existential contemplation underpins offenders' thought experiments and, ultimately, their decisions and choices, not just their decisions to embark or stay on the criminal path, but also their choosing to desist from offending (e.g. Farrall, 2005). This literature also attempts to explore how policy makers and institutional practitioners active in the criminal justice system or in government administrations make decisions, and how *their* choices often preclude alternative ways of dealing with crime and unwelcome behaviour. This emerging literature, however, has its precursors. David Matza, discussed earlier, published an important book in 1969. In his *Becoming Deviant* (note the word *becoming* in the title) Matza was at pains to illustrate how, through constant and minute deliberations, people choose to take part in particular activities which are deemed or defined as 'criminal', while on other occasions they may decide to stay clear of such activities altogether. In other words: people *are* not criminal, they are not criminals. They decide to commit particular offences, or decide to give them up temporarily, following intricate contemplation and consideration of their perceived relation to others and the interactions they have or are involved in. Crime, or deviancy more generally, is a matter of becoming, of ever-ongoing becoming. There is nothing predetermined, nothing mechanistic about crime and deviance.

Becoming deviants, as we have seen, do take account of what others say and do, or might be thinking about them. They do take account of what parents and friends say and do. They contemplate words spoken by police officers, magistrates and judges, probation officers, and other figures of authority. They mull over these words before they make decisions and choices the outcome of which – let us repeat here – is uncertain. It is part of a criminologist's job, claims Matza, to find out about such processes of becoming deviant. Since *definitions of the situation* by officials (e.g. state officials, or the state as such) are part and parcel of what becoming deviants (and that includes all of us) deliberate and decide upon, criminologists also need to think about how officialdom, or how the state as such choose to construct and word their definitions of the situation. These definitions are also based on deliberations, on decisions and on choices.

Let us illustrate this at micro-level, using the example of an everyday scene which some of us may have witnessed on a Saturday night. Picture yourself a police officer who stumbles across a group of drunken women who hurl abuse at him. The officer's fundamental choice (his life project) leads him to want to be, or at least to come across, not as a 'crime fighter' but, rather, as a gentle, humane and sensitive 'social worker'. Above all he wants to be respected and admired, and at some point in his life he chose the 'social worker' route above the 'crime fighting' one to achieve just that. But the women's abuse is growing ever-stronger, and stones and sticks are picked up and thrown his way. A crowd of bystanders is gathering. In turn they are beginning to jeer at the policeman whom they call names for not sorting out the women more firmly. How is the officer going to react to their definition of the situation? How is *he* going to define the situation in turn? Is he going to try to defuse the situation amicably, with lots of humour? Or are we going to end up with another 'violent crime' statistic in the books, the officer's cherished 'social worker' image notwithstanding? There is nothing mechanistic about such deliberations and choices, and their outcome may go in a number of directions. They are fully immersed in processes of interaction and becoming. They are part of chains of action and reaction. All definitions of the situation generated and exchanged in these chains will be reductions of the full potential of being. *As* reductions they are bound to prompt further contemplation and yet further reductive reactions. This is just an everyday scene. But reductive chains of action and reaction could also be established as the basic dynamic through which policy, including state policy, comes about.

To rephrase all this using words from our introductory chapter: crime cannot be studied without simultaneously also analysing crime control (e.g. in the workings of the state), and vice versa: crime control cannot be studied as an isolated topic. In his *Becoming Deviant*, Matza stressed the need for criminologists to have a closer look at the state (i.e. the location *par excellence* where the label 'crime' is produced and applied), and crime control more generally, but left most of the work to others. Others have taken it upon themselves to contribute to a critical study of the state and crime control. The next chapter shall be devoted to the issue of crime control.

4

Controlling Crime

(on the Mastery of Others)

▰▰▰ keeping *becoming* in check

Let us first recapitulate what we have been exploring so far. At the heart of human existence lies indeterminacy. Human existence comes about through this very indeterminacy. This becoming of human existence, in the final instance, occurs through choice. It is through choice that human being realizes its potential, and that human beings realize theirs. But all choice implies reduction: choice is selective. That means – this may sound very tragic – that as soon as human potential is realized, i.e. through choice, it is also, in the very same moment of choice, reduced to a selection of what it could or might have been. Moreover, reduction and selection in choice means that no chosen interpretation, path or course of action is ever going to be able to completely close off the hole of indeterminacy at the heart of human existence. Only some aspects are chosen. Only some potential is realized. The rest is not, but will remain available, *as* potential. Newness, change and further becoming always remain a possibility. On a more individual level one will find something similar: no decision or choice made by the self is going to be able to close the hole of indeterminacy at its very heart. As long as the self is able to distance itself from itself, monitor itself, and contemplate its position in the world, no choice or series of choices is going to be able to stop the possibility of further choice, and change.

As selection and reduction, choice always carries within itself the potential for conflict. If human life becomes through endless and unstoppable chains of minute choices and counter-choices, each of which by its very nature carrying potential conflict, then one may not hope for a fully universal, completely harmonious humanity. Humanity is always going to be marked by diversity, and much of this diversity is always going to be ridden with conflict. Let us think this through. If humanity comes into existence through choice, then any fully harmonious humanity (if it is possible to imagine such a thing) would also have to come into existence through choice. But that means that by its very nature it would only be able to maintain itself, quite paradoxically so, by means of a conflict which keeps at bay or neutralizes that which was *not* chosen. Human conflict, or better, the potential for human conflict, is ineradicable. At any given time, or in any given society, there are always going to be actions that will be unwelcome for some. Some of those actions may get to be defined as 'crimes' and form the object of crime control efforts which, in turn, will tend to provide a source of further actions and reactions perceived as unwelcome (by some at least).

Rulers and governors or ruling elites more broadly have, through the ages, tried to stem the ineradicable stream of becoming that keeps pouring out of human being's and beings' indeterminate core. At the very least they made attempts to make human becoming and therefore human existence as such more or less predictable. In other words, much of what ruling elites have been envisaging throughout history, and still are, could be seen as attempts to steer human will onto more predictable paths. There are many ways to try to attain greater predictability. One way consists of attempts to expand individuals' material and cultural horizon, e.g. through welfare and education. With individuals having 'more' to survey and ponder, the likelihood of them choosing more predatory or unwelcome options (e.g. crime, or rebellion), it is then hoped, might be reduced. This basic reasoning underpinned much of what went under the name of 'welfare state'. However, as we have already seen, the welfare state never stopped people from surveying and contemplating the context of their relative deprivation.

One could also try to influence the *way* people tend to survey their own being-in-the-world, their interpretations of that which they survey, their internal deliberations, and so on. This could be done through schooling, through moral persuasion, through affection, and so on, or, in a more *herd-like* manner, through the force of example. The aim would then be to guide human will, born out of indeterminacy, towards more or less pre-structured courses of action. In other words, the aim would be to provide people with only a limited set of interpretations and courses of action, and to ultimately make them choose only one or a few 'acceptable' ones. For the best part of human history though, attempts by ruling elites to control popular behaviour and actions simply boiled down to sheer physical force and the threat of terror which, it was (and still is) often believed, provide the quickest way to conformity.

Having said that, let us remind ourselves of the herd-like mentality of many who, for a number of reasons such as a desire to belong or a desire for safety and security, are usually quite happy to choose to follow others in their trodden tracks and deem themselves 'righteous' for doing so. Sartre, in a Nietzschean vein, once made the point that many who think themselves righteous are merely conformist, and are so because they fear the inherent potential for change in human existence. They fear openness and indeterminacy. They fear the inescapable responsibility for their own choices and actions. By projecting their fears onto others who are non-conformist, or different, or *creative* (to use Nietzschean words) they then attempt to attain, within themselves, a certain stability, or calm. Criminalization of others, or their actions, as we have seen, is one of the ways the 'righteous' use to alleviate their own fears or, worse perhaps, their *envy* of those who dare to be different and creative. Joining the great 'righteous' conformity is another way. So, on the whole, one should not be surprised to find that most people tend to conform, most of the time, to that which is deemed acceptable.

Their conformity however is a choice, and choice always and inevitably flows from indeterminacy which, again inevitably, carries within itself the potential for the new. This indeterminacy includes possibilities that allow people to choose otherwise should they decide to do so. Let us remember how human beings, out of the very same herd-like mentality which we already have touched upon, may decide to resist or react against dominant forms of thought or action and indeed choose non-conformity instead. As herd-like creatures, humans want to be admired by the herd, and sometimes they aim to acquire such admiration by choosing to act rebellious or riotous which, they hope, will make them 'look good'. It is this constant potential for non-conformity, dissent, resistance, or rebellion which successive ruling and governing elites have tried to control, that is, anticipate, deflect, steer or guide, harness and put to use, or simply and brutally block off.

machines of control

This chapter reviews a number of ideas, strategies and policies pertaining to such control. In many cases such attempts were presented as ways to control 'crime'. 'Crime' then was often the name given to unwanted or unacceptable (to the ruling and governing elites at least) behaviours, or forms or ways of life. One of the common features of so many strategies or policies of 'crime control' is their desire to make human behaviour and the choices on which it is based more mechanistic, that is, more like the working and functioning of a machine. Machines are more or less predictable. They follow predetermined rules or guidelines and operate on the basis of only a limited and therefore controllable number of principles. The control of human becoming, and the control of 'crime' in particular, have, historically, often betrayed a desire to reduce that which is typically human, i.e. indeterminacy, and replace it, wholly or partially, with mechanical (if A–A'–A" then B'–B'–B") predictability. The ultimate dream of rulers or governors of course is the impossible, i.e. to close the gap or hole of indeterminacy at the heart of human existence and of human beings completely. If that were possible, it would represent the most formidable of feats. It would mean the destruction of what is human in human beings, i.e. their capacity to distance themselves from themselves, that is, to monitor themselves in their surrounding world, to imagine their own position aesthetically and morally, to deliberate upon it, to draw conclusions, to harbour motives, to make strategic and tactical plans, to aim for goals, to change tack, to transform their own self if they think fit, and so on. Above all such radical control of human existence would imply the eradication of *life projects* in human beings. If all this human capacity were to be destroyed, humans would be reduced to their physical or biological substrate. Or they would have been transformed into machines, or automatons. Should this impossible dream ever become true, then human existence, and that implies human history, or simply *future*, would grind to a halt. This is an impossible dream: human life and human future *will* burst forth.

Impossible a dream it may be, a dream it often *has* been, and still is, albeit that the aspirations of ruling elites were usually, though not always, less radical than the dream of achieving a society of machines. Their aspirations were much more about limiting or controlling the theoretically limitless and therefore unpredictable flow of possible interpretations, deliberations, or life projects which human beings might be willing to access, or engage in. It was, and remains, much more about influencing people's choices. As we will see later, many control strategies or *machines of control*, if you wish, aim to influence people's desires, wishes and ultimately, their choices. If that proves to be impossible, then the aim tends to be to find out about such desires and wishes in order to guide or seduce them or, if that doesn't work, to force them towards more acceptable choices and courses of action.

In this need for rulers or governing elites to at least 'find out about' people's desires and wishes one might perhaps be able to descry a kernel, however tiny, of democratic sentiment. One way of 'finding out' about popular desire is to find out about people's aspirations. Any such attempt to find out, to be sure, will have ethical implications (there are e.g. issues of privacy) as well as practical ones (people often strategically choose to hide their true colours behind a smokescreen of acceptable discourse). But if one is to devise and implement a machine of control in order to be able to somehow keep the restless *becoming* of human existence in check, if not at bay, then some implement through which those who govern set out to 'find out' about the aspirations of those who are governed will be required. Even a coolly calculating political theorist such as Niccolo Machiavelli (1469–1527), who never had any qualms at all about proposing harsh and even brutal political intervention if practical political necessity so required, nevertheless maintained that the efficient control of populations (or 'the multitude') could never be achieved through physical force and terror alone. On the contrary, he argued, in his posthumously published *Discourses on Livy* [1531], the most effective and efficient forms of control are built on what is basically a democratic sentiment, i.e. that rulers take the multitude's aspirations and wishes into account. It is impossible to rule, and keep ruling, *against* the multitude. One must rule *with* the multitude, even if the basic Machiavellian strategy is to deflect the multitude's aspirations and steer them onto 'acceptable' paths. The Florentine theorist was certainly not the first to recognize this. Machiavelli sought inspiration in Ancient Rome and its republican institutions and traditions.

And he certainly wasn't the last. When, for example, during the 1970s huge swathes of the British 'working class' were growing anxious and insecure about their employment and about their daily or weekly income, Conservative political elites took these feelings of malaise and insecurity very seriously, for one cannot rule *against* the multitude. However, they gradually steered them onto a terrain and towards solutions they deemed to be more appropriate, acceptable and less costly. The UK Conservative Party not only managed to take 1970s popular sentiment and anxiety about the economy and welfare seriously. More importantly, they also succeeded in sapping popular feelings of unease and widespread discontent by proposing quite authoritarian law and order policies ('It's the criminals and muggers who are causing all our problems') while also pleading for a kind of 'Do-it-Yourself culture' of entrepreneurialism ('Dependency on dole and other benefits and allowances will never get this country on its feet again, only dynamic entrepreneurship and self-reliance will'). Their *definition of the situation* won the day (see e.g. Hall et al., 1978; McKay, 1994), and in 1979 they were voted in office under Mrs Thatcher's leadership. Let us now have a closer, if certainly not exhaustive, look at history.

a constant principle

Around the time of the first Chinese emperor (third century BC) a Confucian philosopher, Hsun Tzu, advised rulers to organize their governance around what he called a 'constant principle'. A follower of the sixth century (BC of course) Chinese philosopher-cum-administrator Confucius, Hsun Tzu accepted the basic tenets of the old master's doctrine. Those tenets prescribed the administration of governance to be a task for professionals who should build impersonal bureaucracies and implement regular procedures and processes as their main tool for supporting and maintaining hierarchical rule, political stability and social order. Hsun Tzu himself tried to build on this doctrine, and did so in a way that, as we shall see, comes across as strikingly modern. In one of his many essays, on 'The Regulations of a King', he claimed that the ultimate aim of governance is to produce subjects who know how to act in any particular situation. Chaos and unpredictability should be avoided at all cost. The best way to arrive at that goal is to install in every subject what he calls 'ritual principles'. By that he meant a sense of and adherence to order and hierarchy. Both are inextricably linked: without order, hierarchy will collapse. Without hierarchy, there will never be order. Hsun Tzu then goes on to argue for what we might perhaps call an embryonic system of rewards (for conform behaviour) and punishments (for non-conform behaviour), and introduces notions of proportionality in punishment. Without such a system, and without proportionality, stable governance is bound to end in favouritism, in arbitrariness, and ultimately in unfairness, and *that* in turn may stir the criminal element to rear its head, as will revolt and rebellion, and eventually sheer chaos.

The bureaucrats who are charged with the administration of these 'ritual principles' must do so with complete impartiality. Governance and control are to be conducted in and through utterly impersonal rules and procedures, indeed: 'rituals'. No emotional or other attachments should be allowed to cloud the governors' judgment. Their judgment should follow 'a constant principle' of impersonal, machine-like adjudication. Hsun Tzu makes a strong plea for 'fixed judgment', that is, for the application of tariffs. This is an idea that would forcefully resurface much later, i.e. in the eighteenth century AD. We will get back to that later, but here is the place to note that a system of tariffs in adjudication has something mechanical or *machinic* about it. The ancient Chinese ruling elite, by the way, had a certain fondness for all kinds of mechanical clockwork and machinery. A tariff system rests on a list of pre-structured and predetermined penalties or punishments for specified crimes or infractions which magistrates or judges, or governors more generally (before the eighteenth century there was little difference between these terms), are obliged to adhere to strictly. A tariff is a *machine* of control par excellence. To a large extent it eliminates the adjudicator's human features, replacing them with a more or less mechanistic logic, i.e. if A (e.g. robbery) then B (e.g. 25 whiplashes). Hsun Tzu believed that a mode of governance structured around 'a constant principle', that is, around inflexible, unchanging procedures, rules and rituals, should in turn be able to produce subjects who would gradually not only adopt the near clockwork-like regularity embedded in these procedures, rules and rituals, but also mimic them manifestly in their own everyday attitudes, habits and routines. And that should all the more be the case if the governing adjudicators are (perceived to be) partial to none, apart from, of course, the impersonal *machinery* of governance itself.

Hsun Tzu's machine of control may have envisaged a mechanization, so to speak, of whole societies and populations through the application of his 'constant principle', but it did not prevent the philosopher from arguing that governance, however clockwork-like, should also be empathic. Without any effort to gauge the popular mood and to try and establish what it is that ordinary subjects want, when they feel safe or secure, and when they live in fear, and so on, and without any attempt to take all this into account, governance is destined to fail and end in chaos. Governance, if it is to be effective and efficient, needs balance and harmony between the constant principle on the one hand and empathy on the other. It is moreover imperative, claims Hsun Tzu, that governance avoid all kinds of change and experimentation. Only rules and methods tested and proven by tradition should be allowed. Hsun Tzu's 'Regulations of a King' betray a deep suspicion of change and newness. Let us now jump to the seventeenth century, to another age when many were obsessed with machines and other mechanical devices.

the *Leviathan*

Thomas Hobbes (1588–1679) was a philosopher and political theorist who wrote his most significant work, *Leviathan*, against the backdrop of what he thought exemplified the state of nature at its most extreme, i.e. war. The war he witnessed directly was, of course, the English Civil War (1642–1652), but also on the European continent a war, that is, the Thirty Years War (1618–1648) had been raging most horrifically. If, Hobbes argued in his 1651 opus, the basic state of nature is one of chaos and bloodshed, or a war of all against all fuelled by rampant individual self-interest, then we need to devise a system that allows us to transcend this state of nature. Hobbes suggested an agreement, or *covenant*, between the members of the multitude. This covenant would hold an agreement whereby members of the multitude relinquish at least part of their rights to a Sovereign (that could be an individual or a committee) who then should be entrusted with the power to rule the multitude. There is a novel idea in this proposal: rule or control by the Sovereign should have a more or less democratic foundation (i.e. the covenant). Without such a basic agreement between members of the multitude (i.e. those to be ruled) any ruling by a Sovereign will lack legitimacy and authority and therefore fail to realize its aim to prevent a war of all against all. But the reverse side of this reasoning also holds true: without a Sovereign who unifies the disparate desires of a multitude of self-interested individuals it will not be possible to maintain any agreement at all.

The covenant presupposes and is built upon reason, or more specifically, self-interested reason. In order to avoid bloodshed and chaos, the multitude needs to transform itself into a civil society. This means, first, a covenant which will form the basis for the institution of a Sovereign who will then represent the multitude. But although the Sovereign only represents the multitude (the multitude remains, democratically, the originator of the covenant) the latter have also agreed to transfer part of their rights to this representative. Once this transfer has taken place the multitude then must abide by the Sovereign's rule. The Sovereign is the only one who can use violence legitimately. And so he should, if necessary. The multitude, on the other hand, may not resist the Sovereign's violence, since of course the Sovereign's rule, through the covenant, is also theirs.

Hobbes' machine of control, i.e. covenant-cum-Sovereign, has a number of flaws. After the Sovereign has taken up his or its role of representation, and the multitude have relinquished their right to resist, the democratic process, one might argue, could then actually grind to a halt. But there is another problem with Hobbes' model. If the default position of human nature is indeed chaos and bloodshed (caused by rampant self-interest), how will this then lead the multitude to reason themselves out of their miserable condition? How will the multitude be able to transcend itself? How could the institution of a covenant result from what is basically a horrific nature of rampant self-interest? Hobbes himself would argue that it is self-interest itself that will lead members of the multitude to relinquish (some of) it, but somehow this explication does not quite feel right. One century after Hobbes, philosophers produced a new theory or model of governance which, if equally as problematic as Hobbes', at least had a ring of consistency about it.

▨▨▨ calculation

This consistency emerged in the course of the eighteenth century in a number of treatises on political theory. One of those, the essay on *Dei Delitti E Delle Pene* ['On Crimes and Punishments'], published in 1764 by the Italian Cesare Beccaria (1738–1794), is well-known among criminologists. Human nature is not only about self-interested passion, emotion, chaos and bloodshed, Beccaria argued. Being human also means being able to reason *rationally*. If the chaos of passion is to be overcome and its dangerous consequences avoided, then only rational thought and reasoning will achieve this goal. Only the cool and detached rationality of reason has the potential to lift humanity out of its pitiful predicament.

Beccaria, like many other philosophers of his time, had a considerable dislike of 'passions' which, he thought, were much too subjective, a source not just of unpredictability, but also of inefficiency. If a criminal justice system allows for clemency, or mercy, for example, or provides privileges to some groups of offenders (e.g. rich ones), then this will introduce an unwelcome element of uncertainty and unpredictability in the system. So will disproportionate or excessive levels of punishment fuelled by the passion of vengeance. So will the use of torture in criminal proceedings. Not only is it then impossible to predict the future behaviour of the beneficiaries or sufferers of clemency and mercy, privilege, or excessive punishment: will they mend their ways, out of remorse or fear, or will they keep offending, out of undaunted smugness, or again, out of excessive fear? More importantly, the inconsistent, indeed whimsical manner in which clemency or mercy or passionate punishment is often conferred will do very little to deter potential offenders.

The organization and administration of criminal justice and the adjudication of punishment should therefore be regular and predictable, like a machine. At the heart of this machine of crime control, Beccaria continues, echoing the old Chinese master

Hsun Tzu, should be a fixed 'tariff' of crimes and punishments. The list of punishable crimes should be as short and the sentences for each as clearly stipulated and proportionate to the corresponding offence as possible. Actual sentencing should focus solely on the nature and seriousness of the offence, and not on the offender's inner life, or on his or her 'character'. It should be swift and it should rigorously follow tariff provisions. It should, in other words, be as regular and dependable as clockwork. Beccaria's proposals went firmly against the grain of much eighteenth century criminal and penal law which, in many European countries, tended to be excessive, Draconian even. In Britain for example, poaching and other, often minor, property offences were punishable by death. An intricate historical analysis of the social and economic interests and political conflicts that formed the backdrop of Britain's then criminal law, and its application, is to be found in E.P. Thompson's *Whigs and Hunters* (1975) and in Douglas Hay et al.'s *Albion's Fatal Tree* (1975). Such Draconian laws, however, did not appear to deter many potential offenders from offending. Some may even have committed more serious crimes (e.g. the manslaughter or murder of witnesses) in spite of this law, or indeed *because* the law was deemed to be too bloody. Moreover, many judges, magistrates and other authorities may have been reluctant to apply the full force of the law, preferring instead, in some cases, to induce awe for the 'majesty' of law and authority through mercy. Others may have leaned more towards favouring common law practice and custom above the application of legal terror. In the view of thinkers such as Beccaria, however, for machines of control to be effective and efficient, they need to be calibrated meticulously.

The ultimate goal of governance and of the administration of criminal justice therein, is the production and reproduction of a stable, regular and dependable social order. This goal should not and cannot be attained through passionate and subjective irregularity. Only governance (and criminal justice), which itself functions according to machine-like principles (steadiness, regularity, predictability, proportionality, and so on) will, eventually, produce the desired outcome. Only governance (and sentencing), which is conducted by means of an impersonal system (again, a machine-like system) that has purged subjectivity as much as possible from its workings will achieve the ultimate goal of a steady and stable social order. Those who govern or adjudicate should be prevented from engaging their emotions, their preferences, their feelings of sympathy or antipathy, in short, their personality and character, during their work of governance and adjudication. Nor should they consider the personality and character of the offender during their work. Only an impersonal, purely objective machine-like automatic 'logic', cool and detached, should be allowed to run its course in governance and sentencing. Now this obsession with impersonality and detached reason was not necessarily underpinned by some malicious intent or other. On the contrary, in many cases this preference for impersonality flowed from a genuine belief in the ideals of impartiality, equity and fairness, and from genuine attempts at eradicating partisanship, corruption, and privilege.

The hope of many eighteenth century philosophers was that if it would be possible to eradicate all subjectivity from governance, including adjudication and sentencing, by turning it, as it were, into a system of pure objective reason, then individual citizens in a political society and, ultimately, society as a whole would subsequently start to behave in a more rational manner, more 'objectively', less passionately, less 'subjectively', with less chaos and bloodshed, and with more order as a result. Very concretely, and taking the example of the criminal justice system, these philosophers assumed that all citizens are potential offenders who have the rational capacity to weigh possible benefits (e.g. material gain) against the likely costs of offending (e.g. getting caught and punished). A criminal justice system that is built on and works according to principles of rational proportionality and steadfast dependability will allow citizens to make such cost-benefit calculations. Whimsical, passionate, excessive or, in short, *subjective* criminal justice systems won't. So, the reasoning went, once a rational system of governance and justice is in place, it will gradually turn individuals, indeed society as a whole, into orderly, rationally functioning systems. Facing rationality, the assumption went on, citizens will almost automatically start thinking and acting rationally themselves. A rationally calculating machine of control would thus produce, indeed *machine*, a rationally calculating society, and that, it was thought, can only be a good thing, for *rational* and 'objective' calculation of costs and benefits should automatically lead to stability and order and, more importantly, to more predictability. The pursuit of self-interest as such was thereby not deemed to be a problem necessarily, as long as it occurred through 'rational' cost-benefit calculations. Seen from this perspective, cost-benefit weighing self-interest could even be a crucial element in the production of social order.

This interest in rational (i.e. cool, detached, impersonal) calculation emerged against the backdrop of an economic culture that was obsessed with risk prediction and risk calculation. The eighteenth century was the age of merchant capitalism, of shipping lanes, barrier reefs and lost cargoes. This was an age of risk calculations and insurance premiums, so it should perhaps not come as too big a surprise that the Enlightenment philosophers, surveying their world as they undoubtedly did, decided to focus on cost-benefit calculations as *the* model for social organization and governance. If we now hark back to what we saw earlier in Chapters 2 and 3, it may become clear how this focus implied a reduction of the fullness of human existence to what has been called instrumental rationality, i.e. reason, or reasoning that is used with an eye on achieving specified goals instrumentally. In trying to draw solely on what they assumed to be the most fundamental of human faculties, i.e. rational calculation, and in suggesting this faculty be made to dominate human interactions and transactions, Enlightenment philosophers hoped to be able to realize Plato's old dream of bringing to the surface *real* humanity. The human world of chaos, passion and bloodshed that we know, they argued, is not the real essence of humanity. It is only a world of human appearances. The real world of humans is, and should be, a world of rational calculation. Just as orderly laws of mathematics and geometry are the reality that structures the chaotic appearances of the natural world, so is rational calculation the *real* human dimension that needs to be wrested from under the chaotic appearances of our everyday lives. Once *real* humanity has surfaced, life will be much more orderly, predictable, machine-like.

Such assumptions, however, are problematic; not so much because *real* human essence has nothing to do with rational calculation at all, but because human rational calculation may not be what Enlightenment philosophers seem to have been assuming, or hoping for. Human beings *do* make constant rational calculations. They *do* constantly weigh up and compare possible costs and potential benefits. But such rational calculations are all, and inescapably so, human ... all too human. They are made by human beings, not by machine-like creatures. They are made by human beings who, located in time and space, survey their surroundings, contemplate past experience, harbour life projects, plan futures, deliberate upon all this, and *then* decide and choose a course of action. Such decision and choice will of course also have taken into account possible costs and benefits, but it is important to realize that any such cost-benefit calculation will have been intertwined inextricably with perceptions of and considerations about practical necessity, aesthetic and moral desirability, and with deeply held phantasmal aspirations. In order to calculate 'costs' the human self during its internal deliberations is not just mulling over potential physical or financial losses. It is also, and simultaneously so, contemplating what it perceives to be potential aesthetic or moral damage or loss (e.g. 'If I conform to the law and avoid punishment, will I not then lose the respect from my friends who think it looks "cool" to kick up a fuss once in a while?' or: 'If I now accept my father's offer of a well-paid job at his bank, will I not then look ridiculous in the eyes of my anarchist friends?'). There will be phantasmal considerations involved in any cost-benefit calculation (e.g. 'If I now become a law-abiding pillar of society, always helping the poor through charity, then many will admire me for it, but my basic wish really is to live a life, or at least to come across as living a life of Robin Hood-like, heroic outlaw resistance, so which one is it going to be?'). Human rationality is not machine-like; it has very little of the mechanistic about it. It is human, all too human. It is filled with agonizing contemplation and deliberation. The decisions and choices that result from human rationality are human. Human ... all too human.

But that means that if, for example, we devise and implement what we think is a proportionately calculated criminal justice system with matching tariffs, we cannot realistically hope for all potential offenders (that's all of us, you and me included) to suddenly grasp and adopt the 'logic' embedded in those very systems. They will simply interpret this logic from *their* point of view, surveying their world, their past, their future. They will contemplate the pragmatics of their particular situation. They will deliberate upon all this while taking into account their aesthetic, moral and phantasmal sensibilities. Then they will decide and choose.

No 'rational' system, indeed no system as such is ever going to be able to close the hole of negativity and indeterminacy that not only allows, but also *pushes* people to decide and *choose*. There may not be a system of control imaginable that would be able to halt this process. It may be impossible to devise and implement a *machine of control* capable of halting this flow of indeterminacy at the heart of human existence, stopping, in the process, human beings from interpreting, considering and deliberating upon their own particular position and relation to said machine. No system is ever going to be able to stop individual selves from *interpreting,* that is, from attaching *their* meaning, to its operations. This meaning may differ quite a lot from the one intended by those who devised the system. Just to illustrate this point, a tariff system may propose a fixed five-year prison sentence for the armed robbery of a corner shop as a fair and proportionate, indeed 'rational' sentence. Actual and potential offenders, depending on their own particular situation, experience, life projects and deliberations, may beg to differ and decide on what *they* believe is an appropriate response to the system's supposed 'rationality'.

There is another reason why any system of governance or adjudication that thinks itself or presents itself as 'rational' may not always achieve the effects it desires: it is *itself* the result of a human, all too human process of surveying, interpretation, deliberation and choice. The choice for a cool and detached, impersonal and proportional system of crime control is just that: a choice. As is the case with all human choice, this is a choice through which the fullness of human potential is denied and reduced to only a few aspects (i.e. instrumental cost-benefit calculations). Like any other choice, this choice cannot represent the full extent of what it means to be human. Proponents of a system of governance or adjudication which is based on this view in no way express full and complete, or indeed *real* humanness. They only *choose* to define real humanness as calculating, cost-benefit weighing and impersonal humanness. They make a choice when they support such a system. In choosing such a system they reduce the full potential of human being to only a few aspects while discarding or ignoring many others. Unaware of the fact that their choice is reductive, many proponents of this model of governance also forget that the human targets of governance have the capacity to perceive and interpret this system, as they would any other system, as something which was chosen, as the mere result of a decision and a choice. Certainly, some may in turn choose to accept or even adopt the 'logic' embedded in the system, but this outcome is not, is *never* written in stone. If and when such acceptance or adoption occurs, it will do so not so much because this system of governance or that criminal justice system somehow manages to mobilize the deep essence of *real* human being in all its 'objectivity' but rather as the result of choice. From an existentialist perspective one could argue that real human being is indeterminate *choice*. Real human being is *subjectively* chosen human being. Existence, say existentialists, comes before essence.

▧ discipline and normalization ...

Having said that, one should add that classical ideas about criminal justice and crime control, or versions of *classical criminology*, as the above framework of thought is often referred to, have far from disappeared. They remain on the contrary quite influential in criminological theory, research and criminal policy. I will say more on this later, particularly on classical criminology's re-emergence during the latter decades of the twentieth century. Some elements of the classical framework however re-appeared in different guises during the nineteenth and early twentieth centuries. Its focus on impersonality, for instance, or its keen interest in detached and supposedly 'objective' processes and procedures, lived on in the emerging forms of bureaucratic governance and administration. Bureaucracies thrive on impersonality and detachment. Personal characteristics or capacities, or interpersonal attachments and relationships are to a large extent irrelevant in bureaucracies. Or at least they are professed to be

irrelevant. Bureaucracies operate according to completely impersonal and often predetermined rules. Indeed, one may go so far
as to say that bureaucracies *are* those impersonal rules which all
who work in them are supposed to follow, if possible mechanically. A prison officer who suddenly finds himself having to face
unrest among the inmates has to follow impersonal rules regard-
less of his personal characteristics, abilities, or the particular
nature of his relationship with the inmates. We have already seen
that it is precisely this feature of bureaucracies which often
allows people for a number of varying reasons to choose to shed
their own sense of responsibility and, as it were, to hide behind
the rules, especially when harsh or stringent measures need to be
taken. The prison officer may then for example exclaim, 'I did
not negotiate with the prisoners and left them without food for
24 hours because as you well know from the guidelines the pri-
ority in cases of unrest is to secure the premises, which I did by
locking up the inmates in strict confinement'. Or picture yourself
a police officer who puts some distance between herself and a
clearly distressed victim of a street robbery, preferring to fill out
forms instead because, 'After all, we've got a professional victim
support unit to provide decent care for those people'.

Bureaucracies thus tend to reduce the wide variety of choice
and possible options and behavioural avenues, a tendency many
gratefully make use of for reasons which Nietzsche might have
called *herd-like*, and Sartre *bad faith*. Bureaucracies also make it
easier for people, as we have seen, to put their own moral reflex-
ivity on hold (e.g. Bauman, 1993), and to shed their own responsibility onto 'the system' or 'the rules' behind which they would
then hide. As a system of governance, bureaucracy had its heyday
during the nineteenth and early twentieth centuries. In a way the
impersonality and impartiality on which bureaucracy thrives are,
to an extent at least, remnants of Enlightenment ideas and ideals
that were hugely critical of privilege. Bureaucracy also mirrors
and reproduces the machine-like qualities of earlier, classical forms

of governance. There is no mere coincidence in the fact that bureaucracy often gets to be associated with the notion of 'machine'. The phrase 'bureaucratic machine' will sound familiar to most of us. In a bureaucracy, individuals and events are supposed to act or behave like mere cogs in a machine, automatically if possible. Neither the personality nor the dynamic of contemplative inner life (the 'soul' as it is sometimes called) of adjudicators and adjudicated are deemed relevant to the functioning of bureaucracies. Only impersonal rule, norm and process are.

Governance during the nineteenth and early twentieth centuries however should not be reduced to the spread of forms of bureaucratic reasoning and organization. The nineteenth century *did* see the re-emergence of an interest in the inner life of individuals. Not that this interest was new. As we have already seen, thinkers such as the ancient Chinese master Hsun Tzu (third century BC), or closer to home, the early modern political theorist Niccolo Machiavelli (early sixteenth century), argued for governance to be based on a clear insight into the desires, wishes and ambitions of those who are to be governed. During the nineteenth century this interest in the inner life of the multitude re-emerged. It did so quite unobtrusively in a text entitled 'Panopticon, or the Inspection-House', written as early as 1787 by the English utilitarian philosopher Jeremy Bentham (1748–1832). Utilitarian philosophers tend to devise, assess or evaluate particular ideas or policies by establishing their overall utility. In his paper on the 'Panopticon' Bentham imagines a blueprint for a modern prison house. In this blueprint the future prison (as imagined by Bentham) had at its centre a tower in which prison officers or wardens would be positioned. The wardens would not be seen by the inmates who, in turn, were to be locked up in cells placed concentrically around the tower. Unseen by the inmates, the wardens would be able to watch all prisoners and scrutinize their behaviour. In other words, in the Panopticon (from the Greek meaning: all-seeing) the centre of power, unseen, would be all-seeing, while those to be ruled or governed would be seen.

The twentieth century French philosopher and historian Michel Foucault (1926–1984), in his book *Discipline and Punish* (1977), picked up precisely that point. According to Foucault Bentham's new model prison expressed an emerging new idea. This idea held that those who govern should make it so that those who are governed not only constantly reflect upon their predicament but also make a serious and equally constant effort to adjust and adapt, and indeed *correct* their behaviour. If you create a situation like the Panopticon whereby people are aware that at least potentially they are constantly being watched by those who are powerful, but are unable to establish exactly when and where this is the case, the odds are that those who feel themselves under constant surveillance will start to reflect upon their behaviour and their own self. In existentialist terms one might be able to argue – as did Sartre, in his *Being and Nothingness* – that the *gaze of the other* sensed upon one's skin will urge the self to reflect upon itself, and *that* in turn is a prerequisite for any self to contemplate conformity.

Now, we already know that such reflective contemplation will not necessarily, or mechanistically, lead to conformity. Quite the contrary may be the case. But that is not the point here. The point is that somewhere at the beginning of the nineteenth century a fairly new idea seems to have emerged, or at least re-emerged. This idea urged those who govern or rule to access people's 'souls', that is, their reflections, their contemplations about themselves and their place in the world. This new idea suggested that not only is it impossible to govern against those who are governed, but also that in order to be able to govern it is necessary to actively engage the contemplating self, the 'soul', of those who are governed. Without the active contribution of the governed 'self' itself, those who govern may not hope to be able to govern adequately. The individual 'self' of those who are to be governed should be made complicit in its own governance. Governance should be about changing the way in which the 'self' surveys its predicament, and contemplates its place in the world. It should be about changing its soul, that is, about changing the way the self thinks and chooses. Governance, it suddenly seemed, should aim for the *transformation* of the self. The self should be transformed into a willing and complicit *chooser* of its own governance.

During the industrial age of the nineteenth century, a new idea thus gradually formed: the self, or the subject, like anything else, has to be *produced*, i.e. shaped and kneaded into form. Only one century earlier such an idea would have sounded very awkward indeed, for then the self was considered by many to be a mere calculating machine, fully developed and universally at work in all individuals in a similar fashion. That changes during the nineteenth century. The aim of governance then is about producing *normalized* subjects and about manufacturing *fitting* selves. The felt presence of an unseen and non-localizable gaze from the centre of power, so it was assumed, might help to achieve just that. At a time when belief in God's all-seeing eye was on the wane, the all-seeing eye had to be moved elsewhere, i.e. into the heart of society's institutions.

This new *vision* of governance was not limited to prisons. All institutions were to work towards the transformation of the self, and that included the military, factories, educational institutions and welfare systems. However, there was more to control in nineteenth century institutions than the Panoptic gaze. Whereas the gaze worked on the 'soul', the strict regimentation of life in those institutions worked directly on the body. The strictly ordered use of time and space in nineteenth century armies, schools, factories and prisons, and the implementation of strict routines in them, all aimed to instil predictable, and therefore *useful*, order in the very *bodies* of the institutionalized. The production of normalized subjects, or in other words, docility, was then to be attained not just by means of the soul-stirring gaze of power, but also through the sheer physical, i.e. bodily impact of routine and regimentation.

Based on an intricate analysis of the Panopticon and the minute and often very strict forms of regimentation characteristic of these aforementioned nineteenth century institutions, authors such as Foucault later claimed that at heart that century's governance focused very much on *discipline* and *normalization*. Discipline aims to produce more or less docile subjects who are disciplined (and ultimately: willing) to adhere to and accept a particular set of predetermined norms and forms of behaviour. Normalization implies these predetermined norms and behaviour are presented as, or assumed to be, standard or 'normal', not just by those who govern, but ultimately also by those who are governed. This behavioural 'norm' or standard towards which the self should then be disciplined may have referred to the emerging exigencies in industrialized economies and consolidating nation-states. Strict regimentation of individuals' lives and strict forms of organization and time management, for instance, were to facilitate, on the one hand, mass production (i.e. the regular and steady flow of strictly standardized output) and, on the other, the production of fit and able citizens who would squarely and patriotically endorse and support the nation-state.

Now let us think this through. Any system of governance that wishes to discipline the self towards a pre-established standardized norm (e.g. docility in workers who unquestioningly follow the regimented rhythms of their every working day according to very strict timetables and plans) is not likely to rely solely on the physical (spatial or temporal) re-organization of everyday lives. Such physical re-organization may of course go some way to achieving the goals of normalization, particularly if it is backed up by physical force and coercion. But it will become clear sooner or later that normalization also requires *discipline*. And discipline works best if the self to be disciplined is itself also *willing* to choose for the 'norm'; if, in other words, it is also willing to *self-discipline*. Nineteenth and early twentieth century governance, then, had to go beyond the mere mechanics of eighteenth century calculative governance. Earlier forms of governance, in the absence of a projected 'norm', to a considerable extent relied on mere calculation and mechanics, since precious little was specified which the self would have had to conform to, or better, aspire to. The nineteenth century, though, saw the gradual crystallization of a norm which could be presented as desirable: the norm of an orderly, strict, hard-working, docile and *therefore* respectable worker or upright citizen, soldier, pupil, student, or patient. One hundred years later, when he was writing *Being and Nothingness*, Sartre would probably have said that one of the goals of discipline and normalization might have been to provide the self with such materials (e.g. the respectability of a norm) so as to make it choose to re-align its own life project accordingly. This new mode of governance somehow had to access and, if at all possible, knead the self and make it change itself. At the very least it had to make a serious attempt to get to know the inner life of the self, and to understand the contemplations of the 'soul'. There is probably little coincidence to be noted in the fact that many, if not most of the empirical human and social sciences (such as psychology, sociology and criminology) did not emerge fully-fledged until the latter half of the nineteenth century. However, the sudden appearance of the gaze in Bentham's *Panopticon* may arguably have been the first, wavering step on this road to discipline and normalization.

Normalization would later take on more humane forms. From about the end of the nineteenth century through to about the 1970s, discipline and self-discipline were often couched in practices and in the language of *re-integration* and *rehabilitation* (of offenders). The overall aim of criminal justice intervention, as it was then commonly held, was to rehabilitate offenders, and to re-integrate them back into the fold of 'normal, decent society'. That has changed once again: in our current age it has become increasingly hard to define 'normal, decent society'.

... and after

History tells us that to devise and implement all kinds of machines of control (e.g. impersonal bureaucracy at one side of the spectrum, and institutions of the gaze and self-reflection at the other) and to hope for life projects to then align themselves within these machines' bounds to a fault is one thing. The actual decisions made by surveying, contemplating and choosing selves is quite another. The self may indeed decide to conform, but it may also decide to resist, or to remain indifferent. Any of these choices could be made out of what Nietzsche once called *herd-like* mentality. The self may decide to conform in order to belong (herd-like), or it may resist or remain indifferent in order to be admired (equally herd-like). The self will not only survey and contemplate its own relation to its surrounding world – which indeed includes rules and norms – but will also scrutinize those very norms and rules themselves and, if it thinks fit, discard them, strive to modify or change them, or replace them with new ones altogether. The hole of indeterminacy at the heart of human existence is impossible to eradicate. It is through that hole that human existence comes into the world, becomes, or changes. The hole of indeterminacy at the heart of the human self is impossible to eradicate. It is through that hole that the self comes into the world, becomes, or changes itself. One may wish to devise and implement machines of control in order to keep all this becoming and change in check, but one may not hope for them to be able to cover up or block off the *nothingness* through which human beings decide and choose.

By the latter half of the twentieth century, the basic machines of discipline and normalization were already on their way to being dismantled or abandoned. The age which some have called 'late modernity' (roughly from about 1970 onwards) saw the emergence of new forms of crime control. On the one hand ideas and practices surfaced that resembled the older, eighteenth century classical ones about cost-benefit calculation. A British criminologist, Ronald Clarke (e.g. Clarke, 1980), for example argued for crime policies to focus on 'situational crime prevention'. Situational crime prevention, which, in turn, relies on 'rational choice theory', urges policy makers to conceive of crime control as the management of *situations*. In this perspective, crime control is not so much about *solving* social *problems,* e.g. through welfare policy or by means of inventive economic policy. Nor is it any longer about trying to discipline or normalize the soul of individual selves. Human beings, in the *definition of the situation* of situational crime prevention authors (do note the pun), are considered as rationally reasoning beings who, if the situations they find themselves in are managed in such a way as to discourage them from committing offences, will, after rational consideration, decide to restrain from crime. If, for example, a particular situation (e.g. a street corner on a Friday night) is under constant surveillance by means of CCTV cameras, then, the theory goes, people on that corner will weigh costs and benefits of committing offences, and will rationally conclude that conformity is the best option. The 'machine-like' character of the classical model does seem to have acquired quite a literal meaning in this late modern landscape of CCTV cameras, 'crime-proof' (or so some seem to believe) architecture, or electronic tagging of offenders. Some individuals of course may, in a herd-like fashion, decide to behave in the full view of the cameras. Everyday experience tells us that others, equally herd-like, tend to interpret the cameras as an open invitation to express their deviant, daring, rebellious self, hoping to 'look good', flashy or otherwise aesthetically pleasing to their peers while doing so. Yet others may simply choose to engage in street fighting a few hundred yards further down the road.

However, late modern crime control seems to involve much more than just the re-emergence of classical models. The past few decades also witnessed the re-birth of very punitive attitudes towards crime. In many ways these attitudes do feel quite pre-classical. Strongly calling for very severe reactions to crime, they often thrive on quite considerable levels of emotionality. In this view offenders are considered not so much as rationally thinking creatures than as biological organisms that must be made to *feel* what we think of them. Although quite different from rational choice theory, this model shares with the former a certain disinterest in the inner self or the 'soul' of individuals. In the classical model there is no real interest in the inner life of the self since the self is reduced to a series of mechanistic cost-benefit calculations. This applies to the conforming self as well as to the law-breaking self. There is no fundamental difference between both. In the *pre*-classical (though currently re-emerging) model there is no need to find out about how the self surveys and contemplates the world, and itself in it, either. There is no particular urge here to find out how the self could be made to wilfully *choose* for conformity. There seems to be no real interest in trying to make the self align itself or perhaps even its life project with overall social norms and rules. Indeed, some authors have recently noticed a trend in the application of criminal law whereby the focus is gradually moving from the offender's 'capacity', including his or her capacity for *change*, to his or her 'character' which, almost per definition, is deemed to be unchanging and fixed (Lacey, 2007). Fixed and incapable of self-transformation (or so it is then believed) 'characters' can only be made to feel what we think about them. There seems to be no longer any need to *reform* offenders, or to rehabilitate them. Mere 'character', fixed and frozen in their being, they are incorrigible anyway, or so it is believed. Deemed to be so completely unlike us – law-abiding citizens who *do* have the capacity to choose conformity – these alien 'characters' tend to be reduced to their mere biological organism. One does not really engage with the inner self of mere biological organisms. One makes them *feel*.

There seems to be something in 'late modernity' that leads crime control to the disinterested and detached management of situations and offenders. Without wishing to define this 'something' or explain its origins in depth, one might perhaps point to one feature of late modernity. It is an age of consumers. Our age witnesses a fully developed consumer society. In a consumer society individuals, rather than create or re-create their self, tend to merely consume it. In other words, individuals choose the building blocks of their own self out of the materials (i.e. things to *have* and things to *be*) which consumer society circulates in front of their noses, on their television or computer screens to be more precise. To some extent of course this has always been the case, but a consumer society such as ours goes beyond the occasional choosing and consuming. In highly developed consumer societies, consumer choice and consumption seem to be the only game in town. Everything and everyone gets sucked into a never-ending process of choosing things to have and things to be, time and time again. This eventually leads to the proliferation of lifestyles and matching 'selves', which in turn only increase the number of things to have and things to be out of which consumers may then be able to make their next choice.

Zygmunt Bauman (e.g. 1993: 139), whose name we have come across a number of times already, once claimed that our age knows two fundamental strategies of control. Not that these strategies as such are new. But in consumer society they take on a specific form. The first is *seduction*: consumers are seduced into society through consumption. Those who are able to consume responsibly (i.e. by making the right choices and without causing too much trouble) should be allowed to take part in consumer society. Those who are unable to consume and those who only consume by causing trouble (e.g. by committing offences) await *repression*, which constitutes the second control strategy. Repression appears in different shapes and forms and may include punitive (emotionally 'hot') repression, or mere incapacitation ('cold' and detached).

Now this reading of late modern control strategies is a reduction of the complexity of our age but even as a caricature it may go some way to explaining why an earlier interest in the inner life of the self is now on the wane. Spouting a constant stream of lifestyles to choose from, a fully developed consumer society such as ours no longer projects a clearly defined 'normal' set of behaviours as the 'norm' to be strived for. The French sociologist Michel Maffesoli (1996) goes so far as to claim that in this consumerist age any sense of an overarching 'norm' has all but disappeared. It has been replaced with the fleeting affinities in what he calls *neo-tribes*. These are short-lived assemblies or gatherings of people ('tribes') who share particular consumer tastes and lifestyles, only to give them up after a short while in order to choose another one. In many a neo-tribe there is precious little communication going on, only a mute sharing of lifestyle experience. To be sure, there is something Dionysian, i.e. life-affirming about the often implicit rejection of overall 'norms' and 'order' by neo-tribes. But that does not mean that Nietzsche would have endorsed them: their complicity in passive consumerist choice could hardly be called creative.

The need to steer or guide individual selves and their life projects to one or a few 'normal' lifestyles is less than it used to be in a now bygone age. Individual consumers themselves will now be less likely to invest much time and effort in the construction of a more or less stable self and life project. Their self and their life project now tend to be constructed, dismantled and re-constructed in unrelenting bouts of consumer choice. In a way, the inner life of 'late modern' consumers *has* indeed changed significantly. On the one hand it is richer, since it is likely to include a great variety of diverse choices of things to have and things to be. On the other it will now also be poorer, for to a considerable extent it *has* boiled down to mere *consumer* choice which, to come full circle, makes *seduction* by means of consumption a likely and 'fitting' control strategy indeed.

Without wishing to overstate our case we could note how the above chimes with developments that have recently been described and analysed by sociologists and criminologists. Malcolm Feeley and Jonathan Simon (1992), for example, noted how criminal justice policy makers and practitioners (e.g. police officers, probation officers, even magistrates) are beginning to abandon an interest in the inner life of individual offenders and potential offenders. The latter have come to be seen more and more as representative exemplars of population groups deemed to be posing risk or threat. The criminal justice system, Feeley and Simon claim, is beginning to process offenders *as* risk or threat, to be managed by means of a variety of neutralization or incapacitation measures rather than normalized through discipline or welfare. One does not talk to 'risk' or engage with it. One does not communicate with it. One does not try to delve into the inner self of 'risk'. There is no point in attempts to access the inner self of 'risk'. 'Risk' is not supposed to have any inner, contemplative self at all. Here's what one does with 'risk': one merely calculates and manages it. Another distinguished author, Jock Young, has recently claimed that most Western societies are now gradually replacing earlier forms of control, which were built for the inclusion, integration but also normalization of difference, with newer ones that focus on the mere exclusion and management of all kinds of perceived risk and otherness (Young, 1999).

However, we must now also admit that this picture of 'late modern' crime control is perhaps too gloomy. While developments such as those described above are undoubtedly part of late modern crime control, our current age also sees a number of initiatives and experiments which express a belief in the crime reductive potential of genuine communication. Indeed, there are now ideas, policies, as well as practical experiments in criminology and criminal justice that *do* try to engage the inner life of subjects, and which *do* conceive of crime control in terms of the creative reconstruction of communal bonds through communication. To repeat: one communicates neither with 'risk' or 'threat', nor with 'character' thought to be utterly alien or other. One merely manages it (or them). But one communicates and indeed one *must* communicate with potential partakers of communal life. There have been and there still are criminologists who think about offenders in this way. We will discuss communicative models of crime control in our next chapter, under the heading *restorative justice*.

5

The Resolution of
Human Conflict

(on the Mastery of Self)

▨▨▨▨ the *will* to crime control

Let us rephrase our previous chapter a little. The history of crime control, to a significant extent, is the history of attempts to control and keep in check, or at least make predictable, the unstoppable 'forms of life' (to deploy Nietzschean terminology here) and behaviours through which human existence ever *becomes*. In pre-classical times (roughly up until the eighteenth century), in the West, one could argue, this was mostly done by means of harsh and sometimes spectacular punishment. The irregularity and unpredictability of such punishment is likely to have added to the terror. Uninterested in the inner self of individuals, pre-classical rulers and magistrates tended to interpret governance as the mere subduing of populations. Offenders were often thought of as alien, different, or simply other. Governance did not imply an inquisitive interest in human beings' inner life. Human beings, offenders in particular, were dealt with mostly in their capacity as biological organisms who should be made to feel where and when to be, how to behave, and so on, and, if necessary, physically destroyed. We have seen in the previous chapter that traces of this pre-classical model of governance, in much diluted forms of course, have been re-surfacing in the course of the last few decades. Paedophiles and other sex offenders, for example, tend to be looked upon as utterly alien, driven by vile lusts, as creatures whose being is a mere biological one that requires mere biological measures such as castration, indeterminate incapacitation, or indeed, death.

To the pre-classical model, which never really went away completely, was added the classical one, roughly from the late eighteenth century onwards. This model *did* see the emergence of an interest in the inner life of human beings. But only the mechanical, machine-line, cost-benefit weighing dimension of this inner life was acknowledged. Any system of crime control, and governance as such, it was believed, should play on this machine-like aspect of human beings' deliberations (which were deemed to be the same in all human beings, whether they be actual offenders or not) in order to achieve overall mechanistic predictability. Traces of this model also have re-surfaced in recent decades, e.g. in *rational choice theory*, and in the practical policies of *situational crime prevention*.

A clear interest in the richness of the human inner self only emerged sometime during the nineteenth century, and continued throughout the best part of the twentieth. However, this interest was geared towards the normalization of huge swathes of the population. The means to achieve that goal were discipline and self-discipline and those manifested themselves in the strict regimentation of life, and in surveillance, not just in factories and in education, but also in prisons. It is this model of governance of control, i.e. normalizing discipline and self-discipline, which now seems to be on the wane, although, one hastens to add, it has far from completely disappeared. It seems to be giving way now to the twin strategies of market *seduction* and (punitive or managerial) *repression*.

None of these models have been able to block off the restless becoming of human forms of life. That would be quite impossible a thing to achieve, for it is through unrelenting becoming that human existence comes about. It is through becoming that 'forms of life' as such emerge and come about, including those whose *will to power* (Nietzsche again) have access to sufficient enough amounts of power to criminalize or otherwise control *other* forms of life, and others' will to power. In more Sartrean terms, one might say that the indeterminacy at the heart of human existence, that is, the indeterminacy without which human beings might not be able to *choose*, is impossible to block off or halt completely. No model or system of control could do this, if only because all models of governance and crime control are themselves part of a 'form of life' which will have emerged, itself, out of this very indeterminacy. All models of governance or crime control therefore have indeterminate origins. They result from will to power. They are choice. They were chosen – not always very consciously perhaps – out of a range of alternatives and as such, *as* choice, *as* will to power, *as* indeterminacy, they could never completely stop the further becoming of human existence, however hard they tried (e.g. by trying to reduce human beings to biological organisms or machines, or by trying to reduce human existence to a social, legal or moral *norm*).

Human beings who are having to confront such systems or models do so as human beings, *not* as mere biological organism, machines, or norm-expressing entities. They will survey their surroundings, their past, present and possible futures. They will choose to interpret the meaning, indeed *their* meaning, of the control measures that are meted out to them. They will contemplate their options in the pragmatic, moral or aesthetic light of their own original life project. They will choose; maybe not all that consciously most of the time, but choice, indeterminate choice there will be. The potential for conflict, and further conflict, will always be present. This process is unstoppable, or more precisely, it could only be stopped if one is prepared to leave the human condition either by actually reducing human beings to their biological or machine-like

dimension, or by transcending the human condition altogether by reaching the state of super-humanness. Nietzsche's
superhuman cares little for surveying his surroundings, interpretation, contemplation, deliberation and choice; he just
busies himself with the creation of *new* 'forms of life'. But for
as long as human existence is *human*, the aforementioned
process won't be halted. Any attempt to stop this process is
itself the result of such a process of survey, interpretation,
contemplation, deliberation and choice. It will, itself, have
human ... all too human origins. Any such attempt will
inevitably be finite, able to grasp only a few *aspects* (more on
this in the next chapter) of the fullness of human being.
Destined to produce choices of only limited reach, it will
never be able to cover over the infinite vastness of the *hole* (to
evoke Sartre's term) of human indeterminacy at the heart of
human existence.

If all this makes sense, then it might pay to have a closer
look at these human, all too human origins of systems and
models of control, however indeterminate these origins may
be. What kind of will to power, indeed *whose* will to power
lurks underneath a particular form of life and under the models and systems of control it has sprouted? Which choices were
made in order to arrive at these systems and models? Which
choices were *not* made? Which alternative models and systems
were discarded, ignored, or simply not imagined in the first
place?

In other words, what kind of will to power or *whose* will to
power lost out in the conflict of forms of life and their compet-
ing systems and models of control? Now, reflexive and self-
reflexive questions such as these were often asked by those who,
in the wake of Sartre's and others' existentialism (see e.g.
Lippens, 2008), called themselves *critical* criminologists. The
answers which those critical criminologists *chose* to come up
with have been, and still are, numerous, varied and very often

quite contradictory. This is not the place to rehearse all of them although I will make an effort to say something about this later in this very chapter, when I'll be dealing with restorative justice (but please do have another closer look at the 'Further Reading' section at the end of the book). Having arrived at this juncture though, we need to ask ourselves a much more fundamental question first: can we go beyond such critical questions and do without will to power altogether? And if not (it's not going to happen, says Nietzsche, for the very reason that life comes about through will to power), might we then not be able to imagine a system or model of governance or crime control whose will to power will lead to peace (and harmony), rather than conflict (and harm)? Here we need to turn to another Eastern philosophy, i.e. Buddhism.

peace and the emptied self

One of the basic principles of Buddhist philosophy (which emerged around the sixth century BC) holds that the road to avoiding suffering, or to achieving happiness, is to conquer one's desires, one's will and, ultimately, one's self. If there is no desire, if there is no will, or, in other words, if or when the contents of the self have disappeared, then there is going to be less frustration, disappointment, aggression, violence and suffering. The road to peace, then, is one that passes not so much through the mastery and control of others as through the mastery and control of the self. A very simple idea this may be, it does however merit some close inspection.

To conquer one's desire, will and self means to make one's self as *empty* (as it is sometimes said) as possible. That, in turn, implies one does not identify oneself (i.e. *one's self*) with anyone or anything but instead avoids all idolatry. Nietzsche, as we have seen, agreed on this point. Using Sartre's words, one might perhaps phrase this as follows. If one's own life project is made devoid of all possible things to be and things to have, and if one succeeds in mastering one's desire and will to identify, to the point of neutralization, then subsequent choices made by a thus emptied self should not lead to frustration and aggression. In yet other words, if the self succeeds in reducing the aggression of its own life project (choosing a life project and filling it with identifications always implies a level of aggression in its own right) then not only will the self then lessen the likelihood of it experiencing, at some point, frustration and aggression. In subsequently playing out less aggression it will also induce less frustration and aggression in others, thereby gradually draining energy from the often destructive cycles of frustration, aggression and violence which so often characterize human interactions. Let us illustrate this in very simple words that may sound familiar to criminologists. If I stop surveying my own self in its surroundings with an eye to identifying with what others have or what they seem to be, or with what they seem to be adhering to or identifying with, whether 'they' be the Joneses next door or others, then I will feel less *relative deprivation* and less of an urge perhaps to contemplate and choose an aggressive or violent course of action.

One of the finest introductions to Buddhist philosophy is to be found in the philosophical novel *Siddhartha* [1922] by the German novelist Hermann Hesse (1877–1962). The book tells the story of a man, Siddhartha, who, around the time of the Buddha, travels widely. Having explored and experienced a great variety of different ways of life he concludes that although all are worthwhile, none is worth stubbornly adhering to. None is ultimately worth following. None deserves to be desired, willed, or identified with. All identifications with particular ways of life lead to suffering (by the self as well as by others). He eventually settles near a river where he befriends a ferryman. There he realizes that life, like the river, is eternally different from one moment to the next, while, at the same time, it remains eternally the same. Whatever one does, whatever one undertakes, whichever difference one tries to make, ultimately it will represent only a drop in the river. Although every single drop matters, it never matters absolutely. The ferryman had realised this a long time ago. He has no personal goals or aims. He is there only to ferry other selves from one shore to the other. Like his boat, the ferryman's own self is empty. He says *yes* to all experiences that come his way: the good, the bad, the irrelevant, the beautiful, the ugly, the same, the different. But he also says *no* to any particular one of them. In other words, he chooses not to choose. The ferryman clings to none in particular. His empty self is content just to ferry them across. He himself never forces anything onto no-one. At the same time he never allows anything to fill his self and to bind his desire and his will onto a particular way or 'form of life'. Using Sartrean phraseology, the ferryman's philosophy might sound as follows. When surveying your world, do not worry about choosing what others say and do. Do not identify with any of this. Do not idolize. Decline a life project. Avoid life goals, empty your self instead. When choosing a course of action, choose to say *yes* to all that comes your way; but say *no* to anything that forces itself onto you; choose *not* to follow.

The emptying of the self in Buddhism differs from the denial of self in Pauline doctrine. Is it easy to see why Nietzsche preferred Buddhism's life-affirming saying *yes* and *no* simultaneously to Saint Paul's resentful, life-denying slave doctrine. There is a certain overlap between the Buddhist refusal to idolize and slavishly follow, and the Nietzschean refusal 'to be thus', or 'to be governed thus' (to borrow the words of a prominent Nietzsche-inspired criminologist, George Pavlich, 2001). Nietzsche did indeed appreciate Buddhist thought, particularly as a set of simple guidelines for what he called psychological and moral *hygiene*. It did however not go far enough in Nietzsche's view. Buddhism did not lead to creation, he thought. Although Buddhism affirms life much more than life-denying Christianity, it does not *add* to life. It merely contents itself to float on it.

Siddhartha (or Hermann Hesse, if you will) was well aware of the paradox involved here. In a brilliant conversation with the Buddha himself, the young man pulls the rug from under the great philosopher's feet. If the basic message is not to identify with or slavishly follow a particular way of life, or teaching, why then would anyone identify with or adhere to this Buddhist way of life and to its teachings? Identifying with or following a system which tells you not to identify with or follow a particular system does indeed seem paradoxical. To choose not to choose is still a choice. But the issue, Siddartha comes to realize, is to be aware of this paradox and to accept it without allowing it to bind your desire, will, or self.

Such ideas are of course applicable to the issue of crime and crime control. Take crime. One could look at crime as the result of endless cycles of aspiration and ambition (grounded e.g. in identifications with what others say, do and have), followed by frustration, then by resentment, aggression, violence and possibly crime. Mastering or indeed emptying the self could hold the key to breaking such cycles. Now take crime control. Crime control measures themselves are a part of this cycle of aspiration and ambition (e.g. the ambition to achieve an orderly, peaceful, harmonious society) and subsequent frustration and aggression (e.g. ever more punitive measures or harsher punishments). There is no fundamental difference between both these dynamics. Furthermore, the ambitions and aggressions in one may, as they often do, exacerbate those in the other, and vice versa.

It should then not come as too big a surprise that not only Hollywood actors but also a number of US-based *peacemaking criminologists* (e.g. Pepinsky, 1991; Pepinsky and Quinney, 1991) during the 1980s and 1990s found inspiration in Buddhist philosophy, amongst other strands of thought. One of the basic arguments here goes as follows. If the reduction of crime (or aggression, or violence, or harm) is what we want to achieve, and if we want to build peace and harmonious relationships instead, then the most effective form of crime control is to reduce as much as possible the aggression, violence and potential for harm causation in the control measures envisaged. That, so the argument continues, will lead others to act similarly. Now this may sound naïve to some. One could perfectly imagine those who are controlled surveying, interpreting and contemplating the peaceful attitude and actions of the crime controller in the way *they* choose to. Certainly, they may choose to mimic the controller's peacefulness in their own actions. But they may just as easily decide to interpret the crime controller's reluctance to cause harm as weakness, or fear, or as a sneaky and perverse manifestation of a manipulative will to power. They may then choose to act accordingly. There is nothing mechanistic about human beings. Human beings survey and interpret, deliberate upon and choose their course of action out of a hole of indeterminacy at the core of their being, says Sartre. This here is perhaps the place to note how criminologists such as Charles Tittle (e.g. 2004), a specialist in control theory, have argued that both too much and too little control in controller or controlled will tend to cause or exacerbate problems. A *balance of control* between controller and controlled could perhaps bring about an overall decrease in levels of frustration and aggression.

However naïve though Buddhist-inspired control criminology may appear to be to some, it does continue to inspire criminologists, albeit that the latter now tend to use it more realistically, more pragmatically, fully aware of the need to be more active, and more creative as well, on the road to peace. This generation of criminologists tends to spend more effort thinking through the importance of bringing about attitude change, or community building (see e.g. McEvoy, 2003; Barak,

2005; Arrigo and Takahashi, 2006). This brings us to another point in *Siddhartha*.

mediation and restorative justice

Remember the ferryman? Having emptied his self, that is, having mastered his self, he did more than just sit around. He ferried people from one shore to the other. But let's read this metaphorically. The ferryman *mediates* between those this side of the river and those over there. He himself will not add to or contribute anything to the process of *communication* (because that is what it is) between those over here and those on the other side. He merely facilitates their process of communication. His empty vessel, or, in other words, his empty self, which is not bound to anything or anyone in particular, makes this possible. Although he does nothing much, the ferryman *does* go beyond the mere emptying of his self. He *does* do something more than that. He mediates between others.

We have already touched upon critical criminology and its continuing search for alternative, that is, more just and less harmful and therefore also more effective or at least more efficient (or so it is then assumed) responses to crime, other than the usual but ineffective and inefficient and quite counterproductive punishments meted out by the criminal justice system. One of the strands of critical criminology was known during the 1970s and 1980s – and continues to be known – as abolitionism. We have already met abolitionists when we discussed their proposals to avoid as much as possible using 'dizzying words' (Sartre again) such as 'crime' and 'criminal', as well as the practices based on them (e.g. the infliction of additional harm in the form of punishment). This is the place to pick up this thread again. Many (though not all) abolitionist criminologists ultimately strove to see the criminal justice system abolished (hence their name) and replaced with conflict resolution practices that would allow both offenders and their victims to directly take part in the resolution of *their* inter-personal or communal problems and conflicts. Criminal offences, as we have seen, were redefined by abolitionists as *problematic situations*, or as conflicts which can only be resolved through the direct involvement of all relevant parties themselves (see e.g. Christie, 1977). Any such resolution however requires offenders and victims to communicate and reach an agreement, which for obvious reasons may pose a problem, for it is reasonable to assume that a complete lack of communication and mutual agreement between the offender and the victim was precisely what under-pinned the original conflict and the resulting (criminal) offence in the first place. The resolution of the 'problematic situation' is therefore likely to require some form of mediation between the conflicting parties to be set up.

The idea of *victim–offender mediation* has made quite some headway among criminologists and criminal justice practitioners since about the 1970s. Many propagators of mediated forms of communication between victims and offenders though would prefer to see the effort to go beyond or provide something above the mere facilitative to-ing and fro-ing of Siddhartha's friend, the ferryman. During the course of the last few decades a new con-cept emerged which captures this 'something more'. This con-cept is *restorative justice*. In efforts of restorative justice the communicative process usually aims to urge all parties involved, including the mediator or mediators, to work actively towards redressing (the consequences of) the harm done, and to restore more harmonious or less conflict-ridden relationships or indeed communities. In most models of restorative justice the mediator – very often an official figure, possibly a criminal justice officer or other state official – actively takes part in the proceedings. In many models mediators have the official authority to revert to 'normal' criminal justice procedures in case an agreed settlement between the designated offender and the designated victim (sometimes in interpersonal conflicts it is hard to designate a clear victim and offender) proves impossible.

There are many models of restorative justice. They all share, at least to some extent, the intention to reach agreement through communication. Using existentialist words one might say that one of their aims is to have all parties involved open up their internal deliberations and private conversations slightly so as to make at least glimpses of their own world and experience, including their internal world and inner experience, available to the other parties. The latter may then be able to take account of this during their own deliberations. And vice versa. But the exact organization of communication in all these models varies greatly. In order to illustrate the abundant variety of theoretical inspiration, aims and goals, strategies and tactics behind each of them, let us just mention two. In one it is assumed that the best way to redress harm and restore community relations is to organize a form of democratic communication whereby the rational search for the best argument is likely to lead to a commonly shared position and, subsequently, to improved interpersonal relationships or even community relations. The other model holds that improved interpersonal and community relations best come about through a process of communication whereby the often quite emotional exchange of feelings such as anger and shame, but also remorse and forgiveness, is allowed to play an important part.

Let us have a look at the first model. In his book *The Politics of Redress* (1990), Willem de Haan, an erstwhile abolitionist criminologist, relied on the work of German philosopher and social theorist Jürgen Habermas and devised a more or less *procedural* system of communication geared towards the practical redress of harm and conflict. By the word 'procedural' here is meant that communication should follow a few simple procedures, rather then focus on particular end goals. For example, power differences should not be allowed to play out during communication, and participants should agree for communication to be guided only by the search for the best, i.e. the most *rational* argument. Only under the conditions of such an *ideal speech situation* (as Habermas called it) would it be possible to find, in and through communication, shared positions and agreement. This is not the place to rehearse the many criticisms that have been levelled at this model. Suffice to say here that Willem de Haan's proposal seems to build on a particular tendency of rationalization in late modernity. However, whereas this rationalization often takes the form of mere instrumental rationalization and, as we have seen in the last chapter, the cold, calculated and non-communicative management of particular populations or groups, de Haan, with Habermas, makes an effort to think a more *communicative* form of rationality. The overall idea is that real, rational decisions should follow from real communication, and vice versa: real communication only unfolds if or when rational arguments are deployed and if authoritarian, partisan, or manipulative arguments are debunked. To come full circle: the latter occurs only in and through the very communicative process itself. De Haan's proposed communicative process is open-ended. No particular goal is fixed beforehand. So, if the communicative process leads participants to agree or conclude that their whole communal way of life or the organization of their community needs to be renewed and changed, then such creativity is possible.

At about the same time when de Haan wrote his book, Australian criminologist John Braithwaite was working on his path-breaking work *Crime, Shame and Reintegration* (1989). In it he taps into another resource which, too, has become abundantly available in late modernity, albeit in forms which, as we have seen in the last chapter, tend to fuel punitiveness and cries for harsher punishment. This resource is of course emotion and emotionality. Like de Haan though, Braithwaite is keen to replace one form of his preferred resource with another, more humane one. Braithwaite argues that (local) communities are usually best placed to deal with (local) offenders themselves. Authorities should thus facilitate communication between offenders (and their kin), victims (and their kin) and other community members, whereby all participating community members should be allowed to express their outrage or indignation. It is possible that offenders may then experience feelings of guilt and shame, but that, says Braithwaite, is not necessarily a bad thing. If offenders find it in themselves to express remorse and promise to make amends, and if community members are then prepared to forgive and accept the offender back into the communal fold, then all this emotion and all this shaming will have had *re-integrative* effects, rather than stigmatizing and exclusionary ones. Braithwaite's original model is slightly more conservative than de Haan's in that its point of departure and its point of arrival are more or less given beforehand, i.e. the sense of community, and the emotional affinity within the (local) community. Writers such as Braithwaite *have* on occasion (e.g. Braithwaite, 2002) noted the need for restorative justice initiatives to avoid a strict backward-looking definition of 'restoration'. The undertone in much of what goes under the heading 'restorative justice' does however seem to be pointing to this original sense of community, and to emotional affinity in communities, as the ultimate finality of restorative justice. In more recent work John Braithwaite and his collaborators (e.g. Braithwaite and Braithwaite, 2006) introduced an idea many an existentialist might be familiar with. Communication within restorative justice should introduce offenders – whether white collar offenders or street offenders – to new and more acceptable images of the good citizen or the good entrepreneur which they may wish to identify with in exchange for respect and possibly admiration.

But let us remind ourselves: there always is choice. To choose and accept a new image or to reject it, or to change one's *definition of the situation*, or one's *life project*, Sartre might have argued, rests on a choice made in utter freedom. It is a choice which each of us makes every waking moment of every day. We choose not just 'rationally', or 'emotionally'. We also choose, and simultaneously so, while mulling over pragmatic considerations (e.g. 'What do I really need to do in order to be able to move on?'), and with an eye for aesthetics (e.g. 'Will I look good doing it?' or 'Whom do I want to look good for?') and morality (e.g. 'Is it the right thing to do and do I really care?'). It might be a good thing if more victim–offender mediators became aware of this human ... all too human dimension of choice and communication.

6

Criminological Knowledge

(on the Absurd)

▬▬▬ taking a step back

Let us go back to one of Sartre's basic existentialist tenets. At the heart of the human self, he claims, there is a hole, a gap, or a distance between that part of the self that looks at or surveys the self itself, and the part that is thus surveyed. This distance allows the self as it were to take a step back from itself and look at itself in order to contemplate its own being-in-the-world. And vice versa: each and every time that the self *does* take such a step back from itself, the distance at the heart of the self opens up. We already know that this hole, gap, or distance is filled with indeterminacy. The outcome of any event whereby the self takes a step back from itself is never written in stone.

Let us now focus on this very event, i.e. 'taking a step back', itself. This capacity to take a step back comes with being a human being. Human beings have this innate ability to take a step back (at least most of the time they have), not just from their own self, but from any situation which they find themselves in and from anything which they are presented with. Human beings have the ability to take a step back from a situation, from a theory, from an idea, from a relationship, from a body of literature, from their role in a birthday party, from their very self, and so on, and see a bigger picture. Human beings are able to place anything, including their own self, between brackets, take a step back, and contemplate that which is bracketed, all the while keeping an eye on its surroundings.

Let us once more evoke the notion of *definition of the situation*. Human beings have the capacity to take a step back from a particular view of things, recognize a particular view of things as a (mere) definition of the situation, take another step back from it, and see the definition in a range of other possible definitions, then contemplate this variety, and subsequently decide to either adopt, or reject, or modify the original definition. Let us now bring in knowledge. Human beings have the capacity to take a step back from anything that is presented to them as 'knowledge', as they would from any other 'body', then recognize it as a (mere) definition of the situation, take another step back from it, and see it in a wider range of possible definitions, then contemplate this variety and subsequently decide to either adopt, or reject, or modify the original 'body of knowledge'.

This capacity to take steps back is in human beings almost without limits. Human beings may always take yet *another*, further step back. Imagine a criminologist who in the course of his academic career critically examined aetiological theories of crime. Each time when he prepared yet another research paper on the topic he took a step back from the previous one e.g. in the light of new information. Each time he then modified (mostly) or rejected (sometimes) his earlier theory. There is almost no limit – bar of course the obvious ones such as life and consciousness – to a human being's capacity to take a step back. After the thousandth time, there will be a thousandth-and-first time. There will always be a place outside the brackets from where one will be able to see *a* (not *the*) bigger picture. There will always be other points of view. Human existence comes before human essence: human beings always have the capacity to choose to escape from what is and to choose to imagine and contemplate what might or could be. There will then always be other views, other interpretations, other definitions of the situation, other bodies of knowledge, and so on, possible. Human beings always have this capacity. It is what makes them human.

This brings us to the absurd. Each time when a step back is taken and when brackets are placed, the possibility emerges for that which is bracketed to be seen in all its limitations. Already a quick glance from this *other* point of view may lead the observing subject to see a bigger, different picture and other, different possibilities in it. The original, bracketed object then acquires something of an aura of absurdity. That which once was held to be the ultimate truth, or an unshakable foundation, suddenly appears to be only *one* truth, *a* definition of a situation, or *a* particular point of view which, in the bigger scheme of things, seems to be built on loose sand. Anyone who has spent a considerable amount of time taking steps back may eventually come to realize, like Nietzsche, Sartre, the Buddha and many other philosophers, that *all* truths and *all* foundations – including the very truth expounded here in this very statement – have something absurd about them: they only work from a particular point of view. As soon as one takes a step back, the picture – quite literally – changes. The American philosopher Thomas Nagel, writing originally in 1970, analysed such moments of recognition as instances when one suddenly experiences a 'philosophical sense of absurdity' (1979: 13). The absurd, in Nagel's ironic view, shows itself when life's events, and the aims, goals, justifications, indeed judgments made, evoked, or accepted in them, are suddenly seen in all their *particularity* (i.e. they always have *particular* origins) and *circularity* (i.e. they are invariably made out of only a limited amount of ideas and insights and statements which refer to each other as in closed circuits). Such moments of seeing occur if and when we make use of our human capacity to take 'a point of view outside the *particular* form of our lives' (1979: 14).

object, event and aspect

Philosophers such as Ludwig Wittgenstein (1889–1951) argued that knowledge about a particular object or event (e.g. a car, a theory, crime, a political statement or intervention, victim–offender mediation, jet propulsion and interplanetary space travel, the robbery last night at the corner shop, and so on) is never a straight reflection of the object's or event's natural essence. Knowledge about objects and events is simply a collection of words, augmented with the meanings the 'knowers' attach to these words, when they *use* the words to say something about these objects or events. Meaning, argues Wittgenstein, *is* its use *in practice* (e.g. 1960: 69).

People attach meaning to objects or events in a great variety of ways, and they tend to do so differently according to the particular *practical* uses they have for the meaning they generate or adopt. Mrs Thompson *uses* the word 'criminal' to describe and explain the situation which she stumbles upon in the orchard. The word 'criminal' here, in Mrs Thompson's very practical use of it, receives a particular meaning. The radical criminologist who witnesses the scene (i.e. Mrs Thompson's calling the boy a 'criminal') uses the very same word, 'criminal', to describe and explain Mrs Thompson's stigmatizing actions, rather than the boy's 'innocent' fruit picking. The word 'criminal', in this criminologist's practical use, gets a different meaning attached to it. But we could say that neither of these *uses* is able to describe and explain the fullness of the event in the orchard. Both Mrs Thompson and the radical criminologist, authors such as Wittgenstein would say, are only able to highlight one – or a few at most – *aspects* of the event.

The simple event in the orchard itself has an almost unlimited amount of aspects which, in a sheer limitless number of combinations, could be articulated from an equally bewildering number of vantage points or perspectives. As said above, one could always take a step back. Here this phrase means: one will always be able to look at a particular event – however simple it may be – from a different perspective, and say something different about it, that is, highlight another one or another combination of aspects from the event's sheer infinite number. Put more prosaically, the point that is made here is this one: there will always be *other* ways to interpret an object or an event. Only our human (and individual) capacity for 'taking a step back' and for imagination will set limits to the amount of aspects we may be able to articulate in our descriptions and explanations of objects and events.

Let's take another example. In city X, police notice a sharp rise in registrations of street robbery. A number of theories that attempt to explain the phenomenon emerge soon afterwards. A criminology professor notes how most robberies occurred in the city centre close to newly deployed though unguarded cash points. She concludes that the lack of surveillance in these areas explains the sharp rise in robbery rates best. Another professor notes that most of the offenders who got caught came from an area which is marked by high levels of deprivation and a near total lack of institutional life. He concludes that the considerable variety in the economic and institutional texture across city areas and neighbourhoods, and the recent increase of levels of deprivation noticed in a limited number of geographical areas in the city, together constitute the most important explanatory factor in the crime rise. Echoing an older sociological theory, a sociology researcher points to what she believes are the twin engines of our age, i.e. consumerism and entrepreneurialism which, on the one hand, stir in individuals an excessive desire for consumer items while, on the other, have led to welfare and other state provision cuts, pushing individuals to be much more 'inventive' when it comes to solving 'their own' problems. Another sociology professor coldly remarks that the crime figures are based on registrations by police officers. Crime figures, he states, are 'socially constructed' in series of decisions whereby individuals decide (or not) to see themselves as 'victims', then decide (or not) to go to report their 'victimization' to the police, where the individual police officer may (or may not) decide to make a note of it, or may (or may not) decide to follow the recently adopted policy guideline which says that all incidents of property crime in the street, however minor, should now be classified and registered as 'robbery'. We don't know the reality of robberies in city X, this scholar claims. All we know, he continues, is that the number of people who are beginning to use the words 'crime' and 'robbery' when talking about or dealing with particular experiences, is beginning to grow in this edgy, risk-aware and vindictive age of ours. Or at least in city X it is. A local councillor takes another step back and assures us that the rise in robberies is nothing to do with local economic and social policy. He points the finger at a recent government decision to move dozens of convicted offenders from prison into electronically monitored house arrest in a bid to alleviate prison over-population. Taking yet another step back, the local chief constable laments the insufficient funding of her police service which prevents her from sending 'more blue in the streets'. Interviewed by a local journalist a feminist academic is quick to stress that he did note the fact that nearly 90 per cent of all apprehended street robbers were male, and … and so on.

The issue here is not to establish which ones are the better theories or statements, or the more truthful ones. It might be fair to say that such theories or statements, like many if not most other theories and statements, *do* make sense and indeed *do* have a ring of truth about them (although the hitherto unmentioned theory that crime is telepathically induced by aliens from planet Zog, or by demons and devils, is likely, in today's industrialized societies at least, to raise a few eyebrows). The issue is to realize that all theories and statements about objects or about events could never be anything but partial, able to articulate only a limited number of aspects. It is always possible to take a step back and see things in a different light or, in other words, to see different aspects lit up. There is a problem however when scholars or academics (or anyone else for that matter) remain convinced that *their* chosen perspective or *their* chosen theoretical definition of the situation – and theirs only – is truthful, universally valid, and therefore worthwhile. There is, in other words, a problem when researchers believe that only theories constructed and statements uttered by *others* are reductive (i.e. reducing the sheer infinite fullness of objects and events to only one or a few aspects) or, to use words used above, circular and therefore absurd. Let us examine this problem more closely.

assembling criminologies

Using work by actor-network theorists such as Marilyn Strathern (1991) or Bruno Latour (1993) it is possible to look at knowledge as an assemblage (e.g. Lippens, 2006). One should take this word quite literally. Knowledge is no different from anything else that is produced by human beings. It is fashioned out of fragments of ideas (which the knowledge producer has happened upon), strings of words (strung together in concepts and theories), material artefacts (graphs, petri dishes, journal articles), personal ambition (e.g. the researcher's ambition to obtain a grant, or promotion), aesthetic desire (e.g. the scholar's desire to *look good* among peers with what he believes is an appropriate theory, or his desire to produce a theory which itself looks aesthetically pleasing), and so on. Seen from this perspective there is no fundamental difference between a criminological theory, for example, and a manufactured car, or a new prototype of an aeroplane. All are assemblages that are assembled, or *drawn together* (to use one of Latour's phrases; Latour, 1990) out of all kinds of materials by individuals or by groups of people who, in the very process of drawing together these assemblages, also constitute themselves as subjects, or actors. A criminologist who devises a new theoretical model for explaining processes of criminalization, for example, basically draws together all kinds of materials (ideas happened upon, ambition, her students' research labour, her colleagues' support, a government research grant, and so on) in order to assemble a piece of knowledge. In the very process she will also constitute herself as a researcher. A group of sociologists working together on a project with homeless people draw together materials, assembling a piece of knowledge in the process, simultaneously also constituting themselves as a reputable research group. Once the products are assembled (e.g. the theory, the reputation of the researchers, and so on), copies or images of them will then circulate through the network of subjects or actors (call it society) who, in turn, may decide to use some of those products (wholly or partially) in their own assemblages. And so on.

That may sound like too basic an insight but it does have quite important ramifications. Knowledge, like all human-made products, is inevitably partial. As an assemblage, a piece of knowledge is bound to be made out of only a limited number of fragments and materials. However sophisticated a theoretical model, however learned and erudite the scholar who assembled it, as an assemblage, it will be a limited collection of gleaned fragments and all kinds of materials. Knowledge, then, is always limited and partial. Moreover, as an assemblage that was drawn together, and that helped to constitute or re-constitute individual or collective subjects (or actors), it will be thoroughly social. No piece of knowledge (e.g. a theory), however abstract, sophisticated, or erudite, could escape this: drawn together, it also helped draw together a social entity. And more often than not it will have been fashioned with an eye on *looking good*.

It is difficult to predict how and when actors will constitute or re-constitute themselves, or which materials and fragments they will use when they fashion themselves knowledge assemblages. Having now arrived this far in the book, that should come as no surprise. Fashioning oneself assemblages (e.g. concepts, theories, and so on) is a process which takes place in and through decision and choice. A researcher who is in the process of developing or applying a particular theoretical perspective has a lot of decisions to go through and choices to make. Surveying the limited amount of materials within his limited personal horizon (e.g. the books he has read, the conversations he has had with colleagues, and so on), he has to decide which are worthwhile. Contemplating this he is bound to also consider pragmatic issues and questions (e.g. 'How best to get promotion?'), aesthetic ones (e.g. 'Will I look good when I use this theory?', 'Will my colleagues accept me?', 'But do I care, really? Haven't I always wanted to be a rebel? Well then why don't I come up with something shockingly exotic or new?' and so on), moral ones (e.g. 'Can I really mention the issue of migration in my theoretical model? Is that the right thing to do? And again, what will my colleagues think of me if I do?'), and even phantasmal ones (e.g. 'My secret wish was always to be admired by the masses, so I built my life project around the model of the redeeming and avenging slave, and so I won't now consider theories or perspectives that might be considered as right wing or neo-liberal').

All these minute decisions and choices will be made in utter freedom. Change is certainly possible. But very often researchers choose to stick with what they are comfortable with, and particular communities of scholars who thus come to share the same points of view or perspective have been known to police *their* 'body of knowledge', or their turf, if you wish, quite zealously. Let us illustrate this. In their paper on 'Ontological Gerrymandering' (1985), which stirred quite some debate at the time of its publication, Dorothy Pawluch and Steve Woolgar demonstrated how some criminologists and sociologists of deviance who were inspired by *social constructionism* (labelling theorists or labelling criminologists, as they were often called) failed to see how their explanations of processes of criminalization rested on a rather serious flaw. Social constructionism contends that social reality does not consist of unmediated essences, but rather of constructions (e.g. the application of particular labels to behaviours or groups) through and by which actors attach meaning to their environment and experience. Analysing a number of research reports Pawluch and Woolgar *took a step back* and noted how many researchers concluded, for instance, that historical campaigns to criminalize particular behaviours or groups of people boiled down largely to the circulation of particular labels by sections in society who, for a number of varying reasons, happened to grow more sensitive about said behaviours or groups. But 'in reality', on the ground, in the 'objective conditions' of society, the argument went, albeit often implicitly, nothing had *really* changed.

This kind of *ontological gerrymandering*, Pawluch and Woolgar continued, is quite happy to look at the world through a social constructionist lens ('The world consists of interpretations and other social constructions', as in, 'These campaigns are nothing but constructions'), but, in the same effort, and simultaneously so, also through an objectivist one ('The world consists of objective facts', as in, 'Nothing *really* happened') without recognizing or acknowledging a possible problem. The problem, however, is even more complicated than that (see Hazelrigg, 1986). A basic constructionist statement such as 'The world is a collection of social constructions' is, if we turn it on itself, a mere construction and should therefore say nothing much about what the world really is like. However, on the other hand, the statement is itself also, and simultaneously so, an objectivist one (note the use of the word 'is' in the statement). The point made here though is that many producers of knowledge tend to see only a few *aspects* while unwittingly or, worse perhaps, knowingly ignoring other aspects. Stuck in their *particular* point of view and *circular* reasoning they fail to take a step back and notice the *absurdity* of their inevitably limited knowledge assemblage. Putting it slightly differently, producers of knowledge always simultaneously understate and overstate their case. They *understate* it for the aspects, which they managed to focus on, will never exhaust the limitless multiplicity of that which they produce knowledge about. They simultaneously *overstate* their case, for in focusing on inevitably particular aspects they are placing too much weight on them. However, there is always choice. One could always choose to take a step back and have a good look at one's assemblages, at one's self, and at the kind of academic actor one wishes to be.

7

Afterthought

Criminology, if one comes to think of it, is about the shifting boundaries between those who are 'in' and those who are 'out'. Take gang life. Note how the boundary between 'in' and 'out' is a recurring theme in gang life, where so much of gang members' energy goes into defining and maintaining correct or appropriate knowledge of signs, practices, methods, threats, defenses and, more generally, behaviour.

Or consider the example of a board of directors (e.g. fraudulent company X's) where good knowledge about what constitutes 'good accounts' (i.e. acceptable, or in a sense, internally legitimate accounts) is paramount in any decision which the board may take. During board room meetings one has to be either very foolish or very brave (depending on your viewpoint) to produce *alternative* 'good accounts'.

Or imagine a professional group of victim–offender mediators who spend a lot of time acquiring stable knowledge about crime, about 'restorative justice', or about interpersonal dynamics and standards of professional practice. Imagine how they will be inclined to demonstrate their 'good' knowledge of these issues, circulating it among their colleagues through talk and visual display, hoping perhaps to be accepted by their fellow mediators as 'one of us', or, as the case may be, hoping instead to be recognized as an 'innovator', a 'risk taker', a 'radical', or a 'rebel'.

Now picture yourself in a criminology department where researchers are eager to acquire good and stable knowledge about gangs and gang members, about company X's board room dynamics, about restorative justice, about victim–offender mediators and their professional standards, about who or what counts as ''in' and who or what counts as 'out', and so on. There may not be much fundamental difference between these four *human ... all too human* contexts or situations. The criminologist though may wish to choose to become aware of this.

Further Reading

As I wrote in the Introduction, this book is not an 'Introduction to Criminology'. It merely provides the reader with a slightly philosophically inspired introduction to the study of criminology. I did, however, promise to place some signposts to further readings. There are a great number and variety of good introductory and advanced criminology textbooks available. Many explore themes and topics pertaining to the three basic criminological questions in quite some detail and depth, and most also include a succinct overview of theoretical models and perspectives which criminologists have used to get to grips with those very questions. Wayne Morrison's *Theoretical Criminology: From Modernity to Post-Modernism*, however, provides a breathtaking historical survey of such theories and perspectives. Advanced students should also pick up a copy of David Downes and Paul Rock's *Understanding Deviance*, a highly illuminating analysis of sociological theories, models and perspectives that have been inspiring and continue to inspire generations of criminologists and sociologists of deviance.

In Chapter 5 we mentioned *critical* criminology. Students will find an historical overview and intricate analysis of theoretical perspectives as well as policy proposals emanating from this body of thought and literature in René van Swaaningen's *Critical Criminology: Visions from Europe*. George Pavlich's *Critique and Radical Discourses on Crime* provides a critical analysis from one of the foremost Nietzsche-inspired scholars in the field of criminology and socio-legal studies.

The little book you are holding in your hands has, one could argue, a slight philosophical bent to it. There have not been that many books recently in which issues of crime and crime control are approached philosophically, but Bruce Arrigo and Christopher

Williams have edited a collection that attempts to do just that: *Philosophy, Crime, and Criminology*. On the connections between existentialist philosophy and criminological issues and problems, readers should be able to find more in mine and Don Crewe's collection on *Existentialist Criminology*.

One idea in this book has taken centre stage, i.e. the idea that at the heart of human existence one finds indeterminacy. Criminologists have of late made serious efforts to think through and apply the issue of existential indeterminacy to issues and problems of crime, crime control and criminal justice. However, many have done so using insights from complexity theory (or 'chaos theory') rather than existentialism. Advanced students may want to pick up a copy of Dragan Milovanovic's *Chaos, Criminology, and Social Justice*, and his and Stuart Henry's *Constitutive Criminology*.

References

Arrigo, B. and Williams, C. (eds) (2006) *Philosophy, Crime, and Criminology*. Chicago: University of Illinois Press.

Arrigo, B. and Takahashi, Y. (2006) 'Recommunalization of the Disenfranchised: A Theoretical and Critical Criminological Inquiry', *Theoretical Criminology* 10 (3): 307–336.

Barak, G. (2005) 'A Reciprocal Approach to Peacemaking Criminology: Between Adversarialism and Mutualism', *Theoretical Criminology* 9 (2): 131–152.

Bataille, G. (1988 and 1992) *The Accursed Share* (3 vols). New York: Zone Books.

Bauman, Z. (1989) *Modernity and the Holocaust*. Cambridge: Polity Press.

Bauman, Z. (1993) *Postmodern Ethics*. Oxford: Blackwell.

Beccaria, C. (1995) [1764] '*On Crimes and Punishments*' and Other *Writings*. Cambridge: Cambridge University Press.

Bentham, J. (1995) [1787] 'Panopticon, or the Inspection-House' in M. Bosovic (ed.) *The Panopticon Writings*. London: Verso, pp. 29–95.

Braithwaite, J. (1989) *Crime, Shame and Reintegration*. Cambridge: Cambridge University Press.

Braithwaite, J. (2002) *Restorative Justice and Responsive Regulation*. Oxford: Oxford University Press.

Braithwaite, J. and Braithwaite, V. (2006) 'Democratic Sentiment and Cyclical Markets in Vice', *British Journal of Criminology*, 46 (6): 1110–1127.

Christie, N. (1977) 'Conflicts as Property', *British Journal of Criminology*, 17 (1): 1–19.

Clarke, R. (1980) 'Situational Crime Prevention: Theory and Practice', *British Journal of Criminology* 20 (2): 136–147.

Cohen, S. (1988) *Against Criminology*. New Brunswick: Transaction Books.

Crewe, D. and Lippens, R. (eds) (2009) *Existentialist Criminology*. London: Routledge-Glasshouse.

de Haan, W. (1990) *The Politics of Redress: Crime, Punishment, and Penal Abolition*. London: Unwin Hyman.

Deleuze, G. (1995) *Negotiations*. New York: Columbia University Press.

Downes, D. and Rock, P. (2007) *Understanding Deviance* (5th edition). Oxford: Oxford University Press.

Farrall, S. (2005) 'On the Existential Aspects of Desistance from Crime', *Symbolic Interaction* 28 (3): 367–86.

Feeley, M. and Simon, J. (1992) 'The New Penology', *Criminology*, 30 (4): 452–474.

Foucault, M. (1977) *Discipline and Punish: The Birth of the Prison*. London: Penguin.

Fromm, E. (1941) *Escape from Freedom*. New York: Holt, Rineheart and Winston.

Hall, S., Critcher, C, Jefferson, T., Clarke, J. and Roberts, B. (1978) *Policing the Crisis: Mugging, the State, and Law and Order*. London: Macmillan.

Hay, D., Linebaugh, P., Rule, J., Thompson, E.P., Winslow, C. (1975) *Albion's Fatal Tree. Crime and Society in Eighteenth Century England*. New York: Pantheon.

Hazelrigg, L. (1986) 'Is There a Choice between "Constructivism" and "Objectivism"?', *Social Problems*, 33: 201–213.

Hesse, H. (1991) [1922] *Siddhartha*. London: Picador.

Hobbes, T. (1950) [1651] *Leviathan*. London: J.M. Dent.

Hsun Tzu (1964) [255 BC] 'The Regulations of a King', in *Basic Writings of Mo Tzu, Hsun Tzu, and Han Fei Tzu*, transl. B. Watson. New York: Columbia University Press, pp. B33–B55.

Hulsman, L. (1986) 'Critical Criminology and the Concept of Crime', *Contemporary Crises*, 10 (1): 63–80.

Lacey, N. (2007) 'Space, Time and Function: Intersecting Principles of Responsibility Across the Terrain of Criminal Justice' *Criminal Law and Philosophy,* 1 (3): 233–250.

Lakoff, G. and Johnson, M. (1999) *Philosophy in the Flesh*. New York: Basic Books.

Latour, B. (1993) *We Have Never Been Modern*. Cambridge: Harvard University Press.

Latour, B. (1990) 'Drawing Things Together' in M. Lynch and S. Woolgar (eds) *Representation in Scientific Practice*. Cambridge: MIT Press, pp. 19–68.

Lemert, E. (1951) *Social Pathology: Systematic Approaches to the Study of Sociopathic Behavior*. New York: McGraw-Hill.

Lippens, R. (2006) 'Crime, Criminology, and Epistemology: Tribal Considerations', in B. Arrigo, and C. Williams (eds) *Philosophy, Crime, and Criminology*. Chicago: University of Illinois Press, pp. 103–133.

Lippens, R. (2008) 'Whither Critical Criminology? A Contemplation on Existential Hybridization', *Critical Criminology* 16 (2): 145–156.

Machiavelli, N. (1997) [1531] *Discourses on Livy*. Oxford: Oxford University Press.

Maffesoli, M. (1996) *The Time of the Tribes*. London: Sage.

Matza, D. (1969) *Becoming Deviant*. Englewood Cliffs: Prentice-Hall.

McEvoy, K. (2003) 'Beyond the Metaphor: Political Violence, Human Rights, and "New" Peacemaking Criminology', *Theoretical Criminology* 7 (3): 319–346.

McKay, G. (ed.) (1994) *DIY Culture*. London: Verso.

Mead, G.H. (1934) *Mind, Self and Society*. Chicago: Chicago University Press.

Milovanovic, D. (ed.) (1997) *Chaos, Criminology, and Social Justice*. Westport: Praeger.

Milovanovic, D. and Henry, S. (1996) *Constitutive Criminology*. London: Sage.

More, T. (1965) [1516] *Utopia*. London: Penguin.

Morrison, W. (1995) *Theoretical Criminology: From Modernity to Post-Modernism*. London: Cavendish.

Nagel, T. (1979) *Mortal Questions*. Cambridge: Cambridge University Press.

Nietzsche, F. (1936) [1883–5] *Thus Spake Zarathustra*. London: Dent & Sons.

Nietzsche, F. (1992) [1908] *Ecce Homo: How One Becomes What One Is*. London: Penguin.

Nietzsche, F. (1990) [1889 and 1895] *Twilight of the Idols and the Anti-Christ*. London: Penguin.

Pascal, B. (1995) [1670] *Pensées*. London: Penguin.

Pavlich, G. (2000) *Critique and Radical Discourses on Crime*. Aldershot: Ashgate.

Pavlich, G. (2001) 'Nietzsche, Critique and the Promise of Not Being Thus...' *International Journal for the Semiotics of Law*, 13: 357–375.

Pepinsky, H. (1991) *The Geometry of Violence and Democracy*. Bloomington: Indiana University Press.

Pepinsky, H. and Quinney, R. (1991) *Criminology as Peacemaking*. Bloomington: Indiana University Press.

Plato (1969) [C4 BC] 'Phaedo' in *The Last Days of Socrates*. London: Penguin, pp. 97–183.

Salomé, L. (2001) [1894] *Nietzsche*. Chicago: University of Illinois Press.

Sartre, J.-P. (2003) [1943] *Being and Nothingness*. London: Routledge.

Sartre, J.-P. [1946] *Existentialism is a Humanism*. Lecture. i.e. 'given at The cub Maintenant, Paris October 29, 1945.

Sartre, J.-P. (1963) [1952] *Saint Genet: Actor and Martyr*. New York: George Braziller.

Schinkel, W. (2009) 'Biaphobia, State Violence, and the Definition of Vidence,' in Crewe, D. and Tippens, R. (eds) *Existential Criminology*. London: Roultedge.

Strathern, M. (1991) *Partial Connections*. Lanham: Rowan and Littlefield.

Sykes, G. and Matza, D. (1957) 'Techniques of Neutralization: A Theory of Delinquency', *American Sociological Review*, 22: 664–670.

Thompson, E.P. (1975) *Whigs and Hunters: The Origin of the Black Act*. London: Allen Lane.

Tittle, C. (2004) 'Refining Control Balance Theory', *Theoretical Criminology*, 8 (4): 395–428.

van Swaaningen, R. (1997) *Critical Criminology: Visions from Europe*. London: Sage.

Wittgenstein, L. (1960) *The Blue and Brown Books*. New York: Harper & Row.

Woolgar, S. and Pawluch, D. (1985) 'Ontological Gerrymandering: The Anatomy of Social Problems Explanations', *Social Problems* 32: 214–227.

Young, J. (1999) *The Exclusive Society*. London: Sage.

Index